MW00398697

# HEAVY BAG
## TRAINING

*For Boxing,
Mixed Martial Arts
and Self-Defense*

BOOK 1 OF A CONTINUING SERIES

# SAMMY FRANCO

**Also by Sammy Franco**

Heavy Bag Combinations: The Ultimate Guide to Heavy Bag Punching Combinations
Invincible: Mental Toughness Techniques for Peak Performance
Unleash Hell: A Step-by-Step Guide to Devastating Widow Maker Combinations
Feral Fighting: Advanced Widow Maker Fighting Techniques
The Widow Maker Program: Extreme Self-Defense for Deadly Force Situations
Stand and Deliver: A Street Warrior's Guide to Tactical Combat Stances
Maximum Damage: Hidden Secrets Behind Brutal Fighting Combinations
First Strike: End a Fight in Ten Seconds or Less!
The Bigger They Are, The Harder They Fall
Self-Defense Tips and Tricks
Kubotan Power: Quick & Simple Steps to Mastering the Kubotan Keychain
The Complete Body Opponent Bag Book
Gun Safety: For Home Defense and Concealed Carry
Out of the Cage: A Guide to Beating a Mixed Martial Artist on the Street
Warrior Wisdom: Inspiring Ideas from the World's Greatest Warriors
Savage Street Fighting: Tactical Savagery as a Last Resort
War Machine: How to Transform Yourself Into a Vicious and Deadly Street Fighter
1001 Street Fighting Secrets
When Seconds Count: Self-Defense for the Real World
Killer Instinct: Unarmed Combat for Street Survival
Street Lethal: Unarmed Urban Combat

**Heavy Bag Training: For Boxing, Mixed Martial Arts & Self-Defense (Book 1 of a Continuing Series)**
Copyright © 2013-2015 by Sammy Franco
ISBN: 978-0-9890382-4-9
Printed in the United States of America

Published by Contemporary Fighting Arts, LLC.
Visit us Online at: **www.SammyFranco.com**
Follow us on Twitter: **@RealSammyFranco**

All rights reserved. Except for use in a review, no portion of this book may be reproduced in any form without the express written permission of the author.

For author interviews or publicity information, please send inquiries in care of the publisher.

# Contents

*"Take things as they are. Punch when you have to punch. Kick when you have to kick."*

*- Bruce Lee*

# Caution!

The author, publisher, and distributors of this book disclaim any liability from loss, injury, or damage, personal or otherwise, resulting from the information and procedures in this book. This book is for academic study only.

The information contained in this book is not designed to diagnose, treat, or manage any physical health conditions.

Before you begin any exercise or activity, including those suggested in this book, it is important to check with your physician to see if you have any condition that might be aggravated by strenuous training.

# About this book

*Heavy Bag Training* is my first book in the Heavy Bag Training Series. Practitioners who use this text as a reference tool will establish a rock solid foundation for heavy bag training. In fact, the skills and techniques featured in this book will significantly improve your fighting skills, enhance your conditioning, and introduce you to new aspects of heavy bag training.

The skills and techniques featured in this book will also help you achieve maximum training performance in a variety of professional and recreational activities including, boxing, mixed martial arts, martial arts (traditional and eclectic) kickboxing, self-defense, and personal fitness.

This introductory book covers a broad range of heavy bag skills that will allow to maximize your workouts. In this information-packed guide, you'll find answers to the most important questions about heavy bag training.

All of information and knowledge featured in this book are based on my 30+ years of research, training and teaching the martial arts and combat sciences. I have taught these unique skills to thousands of my students, and I'm confident they will help you reach higher levels of training performance.

Heavy Bag Training has six chapters, each one covers a critical aspect of training. In addition, you will also find a glossary of terms at the end of the book. Since this is both a skill-building workbook and training guide, feel free to write in the margins, underline passages, and dog-ear the pages.

Finally, I encourage you to read this book from beginning to end, chapter by chapter. Only after you have read the entire book should you treat it as a reference and skip around, reading those chapters or combinations that directly apply to you.

Train hard!

*- Sammy Franco*

VIII

# Chapter 1
# The Heavy Bag

# The Oldest Piece of Training Equipment?

The heavy bag is, without a doubt, one of the oldest and most recognizable pieces of training equipment. However, with so many different types of bags on the market, it becomes confusing and sometimes overwhelming for the consumer. In many cases, they end up purchasing the wrong type of heavy bag for their training needs.

The heavy bag is a cylindrical shaped bag designed to be repeatedly kicked, punched and struck by the practitioner. Most traditional heavy bags are 14 inches in diameter and 42 inches in length. The interior of the bag is usually filled with either cotton fiber, thick foam, sand or other durable material. However, there are some heavy bags that can be filled with water (often called "water bags") which provide a more realistic target feel for the practitioner.

The exterior of the heavy bag can be constructed with a variety of different materials. For example, the least expensive bags are usually made of heavy canvas or vinyl while more expensive types are made of thick leather.

Depending on the brand, heavy bags can weigh anywhere from seventy-five to two hundred and fifty pounds. However, the average bag will weigh approximately eighty-five pounds.

Keep in mind, a quality punching bag is designed to take a tremendous amount of punishment and should absorb the most powerful of blows.

Since heavy bags are so popular, you can find just about every type of bag by simply surfing the Internet. However, be prepared, it can be a bit overwhelming as there are so many on the market.

# So Many Different Bags to Choose From

The heavy bag is just one of many types of punching bags on the market. For example, punching bags may also include the body

*Pictured here, the traditional heavy bag.*

*The heavy bag is, without a doubt, one of the oldest and most recognizable pieces of training equipment.*

## Heavy Bag Training

opponent bag (BOB), double-end bag, speed bag, uppercut bag, body snatcher bag as well as many others. This book, however, is going to focus exclusively on the traditional heavy bag.

The heavy bag is the single most important piece of training equipment for boxing, mixed martial arts, self-defense as well as many styles of martial arts. The primary purpose of the punching bag is to develop power in all of your offensive "striking" techniques (e.g. jabs, crosses, hooks, uppercuts, elbow and knee strikes, etc.).

*The body opponent bag is ideal for specialized self-defense training like razing skills, first strike scenarios, choking techniques and even stick fighting training. However, when it comes to developing actual punching power, the BOB is a poor choice. The head of the body opponent bag is too light and flimsy and cannot withstand the impact of power punching. It just does not offer the necessary resistance for the practitioner.*

*Did you know that the legendary Bruce Lee used to work out on a 300-pound heavy bag?*

*"Heavy Bag" is a popular term that may erroneously refer to a broad range of punching bags. For example, don't confuse the heavy bag with its cousin, the double-end bag that is used for developing speed, timing, and fighting reflexes. These light bags are useful and do have their purpose, but they don't hold a candle to the superior heavy bag. In this photo, the author performs a horizontal elbow strike on the double end bag.*

## Buying a Heavy Bag

When looking to buy a heavy bag, avoid purchasing it from your local sporting goods store, as most of these bags are cheap, poorly made and won't provide years of reliable use. The heavy bag is a serious piece of training equipment, so you should spare no expense and look for the highest quality brand that you can afford. Not only will it provide years of reliable use, but it will help ensure a better workout.

Again, you can find a reasonably priced quality bag on the Internet. Here are just a few reputable companies:

- Ringside Equipment (ringside.com)
- Combat Sports, Inc (combatsports.com)
- Title Boxing (titleboxing.com)
- Amazon.com (amazon.com)

The actual weight of the bag is another important consideration when making a purchase. As a rule of thumb, try to buy the heaviest bag you can afford. Remember, when it comes to heavy bag training, *the heavier, the better!* If possible, avoid buying a bag that weighs under 100 pounds. Anything lighter will provide insufficient resistance causing the bag to swing uncontrollably when working out. I use a 150-pound heavy bag in my training and it offers me the perfect amount of resistance for intense power punching sessions.

*If possible, avoid purchasing a self-standing punching bag. While these bags might look like a heavy bag, I can assure you they are not. In fact, these bags are poorly designed and cannot withstand the impact power of a heavy hitter.*

# Benefits of Heavy Bag Training

The heavy bag is a fantastic piece of training equipment that provides a full range of benefits for the practitioner. In this section, I am going to discuss some of the many benefits that come from working out on the bag.

## Cardiovascular Conditioning

If you workout on the heavy bag with a significant amount of intensity, you can turn it into a challenging cardiovascular workout. However, this will require you to push yourself and throw your punches, kicks and strikes at a very respectable pace. Keep in mind, if you deliver your blows maximum power and intensity, your workout will quickly become an anaerobic workout, and you'll most likely fizzle out.

Heavy bag sessions can last anywhere from 30 seconds to 5 minutes depending on your level of conditioning, personal goals and training objectives. Much more is discussed in Chapter 6.

## Improving Muscle Tone

Heavy bag training can also improve the muscle tone in your entire body including your back, chest, shoulders, arms, chest, abdominals, legs, and calves. A typical heavy bag workout can also burn a significant amount of calories and, therefore, can be a useful method for stripping fat from your body.

While heavy bag training does improve muscle tone, it should not be used as a substitute for weight training. For those of you who want to achieve noticeable strength gains, I strongly encourage a progressive resistance exercise program.

*Martial artists, of all styles, use the heavy bag in their training. In this photo, a traditional Karateka delivers a reverse punch to the bag.*

*While regular heavy bag training will improve your muscle tone, it should not be used as a substitute for weight training.*

# Developing Fighting Technique

The heavy bag is also a fantastic piece of equipment for developing your fighting skills and techniques. It is no surprise that boxers, kickboxers, self-defense practitioners, MMA fighters, and martial artists of all styles and backgrounds regularly use the heavy bag for developing their particular style of fighting.

As you can imagine, a wide variety of kicks, punches and strikes can be developed and ultimately perfected on the heavy bag. Some techniques include:

- *Jab*
- *Lead straight punch*
- *Rear cross (also called a straight right)*
- *Hook punches*
- *Shovel hooks*
- *Uppercut*
- *Elbow strikes*
- *Knee strikes*
- *Kicking techniques*

*The Heavy Bag is not just limited to stand-up fighting. It can also be used for ground fighting strikes. This is often referred to as "ground and pound" techniques.*

## Developing Fighting Attributes

Fighting attributes are unique qualities that enhance or amplify a particular fighting skill or technique. They might include speed, power, timing, agility, ambidexterity, coordination, combat conditioning as well as many others.

The heavy bag is an ideal piece of equipment for developing some of these fighting attributes. They include some of the following:

- *Impact power*
- *Ambidexterity*
- *Offensive timing*
- *Balance*
- *Eye/Hand coordination*
- *Footwork skills*
- *Non-telegraphic movement*
- *Muscular relaxation*

## Heavy Bag Training

- *Distancing*
- *Accuracy*

Fighting attributes are not just limited to the physical plane. In fact, there are mental and psychological attributes that can also be developed through consistent heavy bag training. They include:

- *Mental toughness*
- *Self-confidence*
- *Mental concentration*
- *Instrumental aggressiveness*
- *Immediate resilience*

## Effective Stress Reduction Tool

There's no escaping the fact that mental stress can do a tremendous amount of damage by causing heart disease, high blood pressure, chest pain and an irregular heartbeat. It's no wonder stress is called the silent killer.

The good news is, working out on the heavy bag on a regular basis can be an excellent form of stress reduction. Punching and kicking an inanimate object, such as a heavy bag, permits you to channel pent-up aggression in a productive fashion.

## Anger Management Tool

Unless you live on your own island, you will most likely live in a populated region that puts you in contact with many people every day. Add a hectic lifestyle to the mix and you will probably encounter occasional conflicts with difficult and belligerent people.

In such situations, you will sometimes get a sudden urge to respond in a physical manner, but as a law-abiding citizen, you must repress these primitive urges.

Working out on the heavy bag allows you to vent toxic anger in an acceptable and appropriate way. It's no wonder the heavy bag is one of the most recommended items for children and adults in therapy.

*When used correctly, the heavy bag training can be a great stress reducing tool.*

## Inexpensive Investment

Finally, for the people on a tight budget, the good news is that heavy bag training is inexpensive. Essentially, all you need is a quality heavy bag and a good pair of bag gloves to protect your hands. Please see Chapter 2 to learn more about essential training gear.

Heavy Bag Training

# Chapter 2
# Getting Started

# Finding the Right Place to Train

One of the most important considerations when setting up the heavy bag is finding the right location for working out. First, you will need a place that will allow both you and the bag to move around freely. The location should also be a relatively quiet place that is free of distractions. Here are a few places you might want to consider when setting up your bag:

- *Garage*
- *Carport*
- *Basement*
- *Barn*
- *Home gym (if you're fortunate enough)*
- *Open field or backyard*
- *Warehouse*
- *Under a deck*

*If you can manage to clear out the clutter from your garage, it can be a perfect place for working out on the bag.*

*You can get somewhat creative when choosing a location to set up your heavy bag.*

*Heavy bag training outdoors is a great experience. However, exposing your bag to the elements, for a prolonged period, will quickly destroy your bag. Be sure to bring your bag indoors at the end of every workout.*

# Hanging the Bag

Once you have found a suitable location to set up the bag, your next task is to hang it up. There are many different ways to hang the heavy bag, but the most important criterion is to attach the bag to a strong and stable structure that can withstand a tremendous amount of abuse.

Just about every heavy bag will come with four equal length chain links and either an "S" hook or snap link. To connect the chains to the bag, connect each one of the chain links to each of the metal rings attached to each corner of the bag. Then join the top of the chain links to the "S" hook or snap link above the bag.

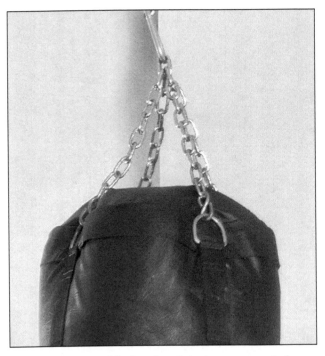

*Pictured here, a close-up of the four chain links that connect to the heavy bag. In some cases, you might have to cut or modify the chains to meet the requirements of your particular set up.*

*To reduce wear and tear on your link chains and to help give your bag a bit of a realistic bounce, I strongly recommend placing a heavy duty metal spring between the hanger and the top of the linked chains. Pictured here, a heavy duty metal spring.*

## Heavy Bag Hangers

Most people will find they can hang their heavy bag from either a wood or steel beam located in either their basement or garage. Luckily, there are several commercial heavy bag hangers that will allow you to hang your bag.

If, however, it's not possible to hang your bag from a beam, there are wall mount hangers that can be bolted into the wall studs.

*Pictured here, a steel I-beam heavy bag hanger.*

## Different Types of Heavy Bag Hangers

- *Steel I-Beam hanger*

- *Rafter hanger*

- *Wood Beam T-Swivel hanger*

- *Flat Wood Beam hanger*

- *Wall Mount hanger*

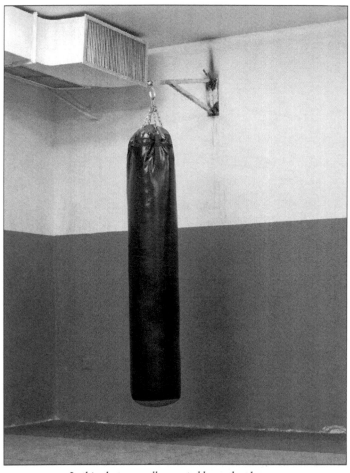

*In this photo, a wall mounted heavy bag hanger.*

## The Heavy Bag Stand

Finally, if you do not have access to a solid beam or a wall stud but do have the space, you might want to consider investing in a heavy bag stand. These free-standing units are increasingly popular, as well as affordable. The only real drawback to a heavy bag stand is they limit your ability to move 360 degrees around the bag.

*Like the wall mount hanger, the heavy bag stand will also limit your ability to move 360 degrees around the bag.*

# Setting the Proper Height of the Bag

Once you hang the heavy bag, the next important issue is making certain it is set at the proper height. One of the biggest mistakes people make is setting the height of the bag too low.

Be sure that your heavy bag is set up so that you can land headshots on the bag. This is especially important for people who intend on using the heavy bag for self-defense or sports combat like mixed martial arts. Essentially, the top of the heavy bag should be approximately 8-12 inches above your head.

In most cases, to ensure the proper height you might have to alter or cut the length of the chains that suspend the heavy bag. This will most likely take a bit of experimentation and some trial and error, but the result will be worth the effort.

*Here's a good example of a heavy bag that is set up at the proper height. Notice how the top of the bag is well above the practitioner's head, yet it's not so high that it limits his ability to deliver body shots.*

*To ensure the proper height of the bag, make certain the top of the bag is approximately 8 to 12 inches taller than you. In this photo, notice how the heavy bag is hanging too low for this man. As a result, his ability to deliver punishing head shots will be significantly limited.*

*Setting the proper height for the heavy bag also applies to the self-standing punching bag. In this photo, notice how the top of the bag is too low for this man. Once again, it should be approximately 8-12 inches taller than the practitioner.*

*This bag is too high for the practitioner. This mistake will limit your ability to deliver body and kicking techniques on the bag.*

# Heavy Bag Safety Tips

Before you launch ahead and start hitting the heavy bag, it's important to go over some important safety tips.

- Consult with your personal physician before beginning this or any other strenuous exercise program.

- Immediately stop training if you feel pain or discomfort.

- To avoid injuries, always begin your heavy bag workout with a light round first.

- Never hold your breath when working out on the bag.

- Always remember to exhale when delivering a blow to the bag.

- Always keep your workout area clear of objects.

- While punching or kicking the heavy bag, make certain that no one is standing near the bag. This includes pets.

- When setting up the heavy bag, always follow the manufacturer's instructions.

- Never workout on a canvas heavy bag without hand protection.

- To avoid hyper-extending your arm, never strike the bag unless you sure you will make contact.

- Always warm up with light stretching before working out on the bag.

- Never hang a heavy bag directly next to a window.

- Before you workout, always check and make certain the heavy bag and its support structure is secure.

- Immediately replace worn parts such as chain links, "S" hooks, snap links and other metal parts that wear out over time.

*Pictured here, a heavy bag station at a Muay Thai kickboxing school.*

- When working out on the bag, always remember to keep both of your hands up at all times.

- Always wear loose fitting clothing when working out on the bag.

- To avoid injuring your hands and damaging your bag, never workout with rings or jewelry on your hands.

- Never strike the heavy bag with full force until you have mastered the proper body mechanics.

- To avoid spraining or breaking your wrists, never bend your wrists when punching the bag.

- Don't strike the heavy bag with bare knuckles until your hands are conditioned to withstand the impact.

- Get into the habit of timing you workout rounds.

- Proper punching and kicking form is always more important than intensity.

- Never fully extend or "lock out" your arms when punching the bag.

- Depending on the type of punch or kick that you are executing, always maintain the correct distance from the bag.

- Never allow people to swing from the heavy bag.

- Avoid lifting your chin and exposing your centerline when working out on the bag.

- Maintain proper footwork and stay balanced at all times when working out on the bag.

- If your hands are sore from a previous heavy bag workout, consider wearing a pair of boxing gloves the next time you work out.

# Heavy Bag Gear

If you want to get the most out of your workouts, you might want to invest in some heavy bag gear. While I did mention that heavy bag training is a relatively inexpensive activity, there are a few items you might want to consider purchasing to help you with your training.

## Bag Gloves

One of the most important items to purchase for heavy bag training is a good pair of bag gloves. Bag gloves are lightweight gloves that offer excellent protection to your hands when working out on all types of punching bags.

Bag gloves are constructed of either top grain cowhide or durable vinyl. There are two styles of bag gloves sold on the market:

- *Mitt style gloves*
- *Finger style gloves*

Some of the mitt style bag gloves may also have a small metal bar sewn into the palm grip area to aid in fist stabilization. Bag glove sizes are usually small, medium, large and extra large.

When buying bag gloves, spare no expense and look for a reputable and high-quality brand. This will provide years of reliable use and will help ensure a better quality workout.

If you don't think you will need bag gloves, think again. Working out on the heavy bag, without hand protection causes sore knuckles, bruised bones, hand inflammation, sore wrists and bloody knuckles. More importantly, it will set your training back for several weeks for your hands to completely heal.

*Pictured here, traditional mitt style bag gloves.*

*In this photo, finger style bag gloves.*

## Boxing Gloves

People often confuse bag gloves with boxing gloves. While the two might appear similar, they are quite different. Boxing gloves are heavier and significantly larger than bag gloves, and they are generally used for full-contact sparring and sports combat competition.

However, boxing gloves also can be used for heavy bag training. In fact, boxing gloves are often used by advanced practitioners for developing strength and endurance in their arms.

The ideal boxing glove is one that provides comfort, protection, and durability. Depending on your training objective, the glove can weigh anywhere from ten to sixteen ounces.

Here are some important features to be aware of when purchasing a pair of boxing gloves:

- To avoid wrist injuries, you want the glove to fit snugly around your hand.
- The boxing glove should be composed of multi-layered foam padding.

- The glove should have a sufficient palm grip that provides comfort and fist stabilization.

- To avoid a thumb injury, the glove should have thumb-lock stitching.

- The glove should be double-stitched to ensure durability.

- The entire glove should be constructed of top quality materials to increase its durability.

- The glove should be relatively easy to slip-on and off your hands. Velcro fasteners are sometimes preferred over laces.

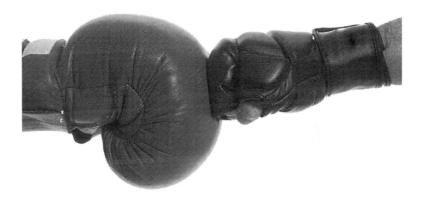

*As you can see, there's a big difference between the bag glove (right) and the boxing glove (left).*

*Boxing gloves can also be used if your knuckles are too sore or bruised to hit the heavy bag with regular bag gloves. The extra padding can make all the difference between skipping a workout and sticking with your routine.*

## Hand Wraps

Hand Wraps (also called wrist wraps) are used by experienced athletes who want an added measure of protection to their hands and wrists when hitting the heavy bag. They provide support to the entire hand and wrist area and can help prevent osteoarthritis in later years.

Essentially, hand wraps are long strips of cloth measuring two inches wide and nine to eighteen feet long. The longer hand wraps are more often used by practitioners who have large hands and who wish to have greater hand protection. You can find hand wraps at most sporting goods stores as well as the Internet.

Hand wraps should only be used in conjunction with either large bag gloves or boxing gloves, do not strike the heavy bag with just your hand wraps as this can easily injure your hands.

Hand wraps are washable and should be cleaned after every workout. Although there are many hand wrapping techniques, the procedures shown on page 34 is suggested.

While hand wraps are a necessary piece of training equipment for boxing, mixed martial arts and other competitive combat sports, I don't recommend using them for self-defense training. Reality based self-defense training requires you to condition your hands and wrists to withstand the impact of striking a solid target.

*In professional combat sports, hand wraps are often used in conjunction with sports tape. However, most competitions will have specific rules regarding the amount and types of material you can use in competition.*

*A close-up view of hand wraps.*

## How to Apply Hand and Wrist Wraps

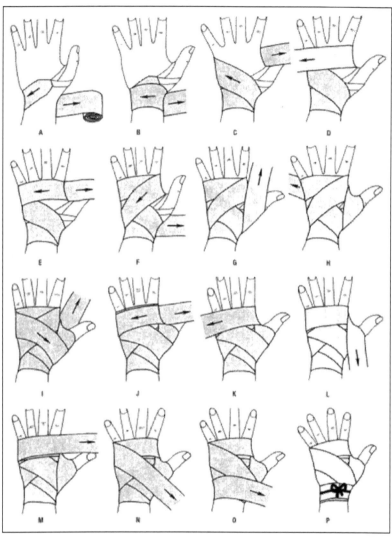

*How to wrap your hands and wrists with hand wraps. Follow steps A through P*

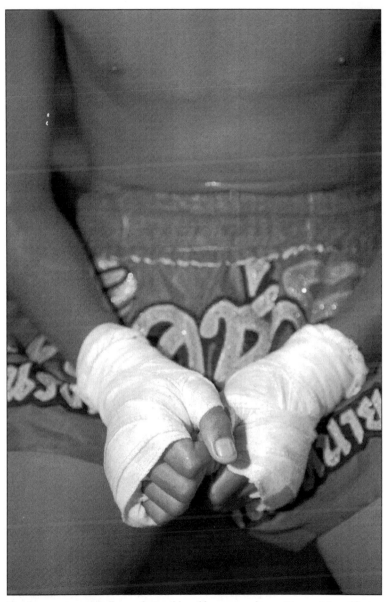

*Hand wraps are used all over the world and by many cultures. Here, a Muay Thai fighter takes a break during his training.*

*Hand wraps should only be used with either large bag gloves or boxing gloves. Don't strike the bag with just your hand wraps, it will tear up your knuckles.*

*Never use weight lifting gloves for heavy bag training. These gloves provide no protection for your hands or wrists.*

## Interval Workout Timer

Since heavy bag training is structured around time and rounds, you should invest in a good workout timer. Boxers, mixed martial artists and kickboxers will use workout timers to keep track of their time during their rounds.

Most workout timers will allow you to adjust your round lengths anywhere from 30 seconds to 9 minutes. Rest time can be set from 30 seconds to 5 minutes depending on your level of conditioning and training goals.

There are several professional timers sold on the market, and they will vary in price. Your best bet is to search the Internet for one that meets your specific needs.

Workout Timers are great for:

- Keeping track of the number of rounds and the time of each round when working out alone.

- Measuring your current level of cardiovascular conditioning.

- Monitoring your progress in your heavy bag training.

- Creating healthy competition in your heavy bag routine.

*One final reminder before moving on to the next chapter. Heavy bag training can be very demanding on the heart. Before you begin any workout program, including those suggested in this book, it is important to check with your physician to see if you have any condition that might be aggravated by strenuous exercise.*

# Heavy Bag Training

# Chapter 3
# The Fighting Stance and Footwork

# The Fighting Stance

Whether you are a boxer, mixed martial artist, street fighter or fitness junkie, you'll need to learn about the fighting stance.

The fighting stance is a strategic and aggressive posture you assume when squared-off with the heavy bag. For all intents and purposes, the fighting stance is the foundation for all of your punches and kicking techniques.

When working out on the heavy bag, the fighting stance will provide the following for the practitioner:

- Speed
- Striking power
- Stability when striking
- Mobility
- Balance
- Offensive fluidity
- Maximizes limb extension
- Complete visual picture

The fighting stance is not only used for working out. As a matter of fact, in actual combat the fighting stance is used for both offensive and defensive purposes. It stresses strategic soundness and simplicity over complexity and style. The fighting stance also facilitates maximum execution of punches, kicks and strikes while simultaneously protecting your targets against possible counter attacks from the opponent.

# The Centerline

One of the most important considerations of a fighting stance is the centerline. Your centerline is an imaginary vertical line that divides your body in half. Located on this line are some of your most vital impact targets. This includes your eyes, nose, chin, throat, solar plexus, and groin.

# Centerline Placement

The proper placement of your centerline (in relation to the heavy bag) is critical and will directly effect the following:

**1. Target Exposure** - A properly positioned centerline will minimize

*The Centerline*

the number of anatomical targets exposed to the bag when working out.

**2. Balance** - A properly positioned centerline will maximize your balance and stability during your workout. This is especially important when delivering explosive combination attacks.

**3. Mobility** - A properly positioned centerline will also maximize your ability to move quickly and efficiently around the bag.

**4. Power Generation** - A properly angled centerline permits maximum hip and shoulder rotation which translates to greater impact power when throwing punches, strikes, and other blows at the bag. For example, try throwing a punch at the bag with both of your feet planted squarely in front of you? Notice anything? There's no power, of course.

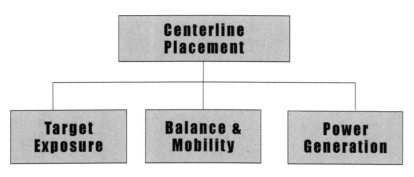

*Your centerline placement will have a direct effect on the following factors.*

# How To Assume a Fighting Stance

Essentially, there are two variations of the fighting stance, the orthodox and southpaw. Let's begin with the orthodox stance.

To assume the orthodox stance, place the left side of your body forward and closest to the heavy bag. Then, blade your feet and centerline at approximately forty-five degrees from your bag. Make certain to place your feet approximately a shoulder-width apart with both of your knees bent and flexible.

Mobility is also important, as we'll discuss later. All footwork and strategic movement should be performed on the balls of your feet. Your weight distribution is also an important factor. Since heavy bag training is dynamic, your weight distribution will frequently change. However, when stationary, keep 50 percent of your body weight on each leg and always be in control of it.

Next, the hands are aligned one behind the other along your centerline. The lead arm is held high and bent at approximately 90 degrees. The rear arm is kept back by the chin. Arranged this way, the hands not only protect the upper centerline but also allow quick deployment of your punches as well as other striking techniques.

When holding your guard, do not tighten your shoulder or arm muscles prior to striking. Stay relaxed and loose. Finally, keep your chin slightly angled down. This diminishes target size and reduces the likelihood of a paralyzing blow to your chin or a lethal strike to your throat during an actual self-defense encounter.

If you want to assume a southpaw fighting stance, you would perform the very same steps mentioned above but with your right side facing forward and closest to the bag. Generally, most right handed people with use the orthodox stance, while left handed people will opt for the southpaw.

*The Orthodox Fighting Stance.*      *The Southpaw Fighting Stance.*

## Heavy Bag Training

However, for those who are interested in reality based self-defense, you must be able to fight your adversary with equal ability on both the right and left sides of your body. This means that you would need to practice heavy bag work from both the southpaw and orthodox stances.

The best method for practicing your fighting stance is in front of a full-length mirror. Place the mirror in an area that allows sufficient room for movement; a garage or basement is perfect. Stand in front of the mirror, far enough away to see your entire body. Stand naturally with your arms relaxed at your sides. Now close your eyes and quickly assume your fighting stance. Open your eyes and check for flaws. Look for low hand guards, improper foot positioning or body angle, rigid shoulders and knees, etc. Drill this way repeatedly, working from both the right and left side. Practice this until your fighting stance becomes second nature.

*One common mistake beginners make is to stand squarely in front of the heavy bag without regard to their stance. Never stand squarely in front of the heavy bag. Not only will this expose your centerline targets, it also diminishes your balance, inhibits efficient footwork, and minimizes your reach.*

*A full-length mirror can also be used for shadow boxing training. Shadow boxing is the creative deployment of offensive and defensive techniques and maneuvers against an imaginary opponent.*

*Pictured here, one of Mr. Franco's students warming up in front of the mirror before his heavy bag workout.*

*Pictured here, the classic "boxer's stance." Notice how the fighter's centerline is angled at approximately 45-degrees.*

*Avoid the tendency to let both your elbows flair out to the sides. This type of elbow positioning places your hands out of proper body mechanic alignment.*

# Fighting Stance Review

CHIN ANGLED DOWN

HANDS HELD UP

TORSO BLADED

ELBOWS TUCKED IN

KNEES BENT

FEET SHOULDER-WIDTH APART

FEET PARALLEL

# You'll Need to Move Around the Bag!

Now that we have the fighting stance covered, it's time to talk about mobility and footwork. One of the biggest mistakes beginners make when working out on the heavy bag, is to just stand in front of it and beat it to death! While this methodology might have some limited street fighting applications, it should not be your sole method of training on the bag. Remember, the heavy bag must swing freely, and this means that you must also be able to move with it.

# Footwork & Mobility

I define mobility as the ability to move your body quickly and freely, which is accomplished through basic footwork. The safest footwork involves quick, economical steps performed on the balls of your feet, while you remain relaxed and balanced. Keep in mind that balance is one of the most important considerations when working out on the heavy bag.

Basic footwork can be used for both offensive and defensive purposes, and it is structured around four general directions: forward, backward, right, and left. However, always remember this footwork rule of thumb: *Always move the foot closest to the direction you want to go first, and let the other foot follow an equal distance.* This prevents cross-stepping, which can be disastrous in a high-risk combat situation.

## Basic Footwork Movements

**1. Moving forward (advance)**- from your fighting stance, first move your front foot forward (approximately 12 inches) and then move your rear foot an equal distance.

**2. Moving backward (retreat)** - from your fighting stance, first move your rear foot backward (approximately 12 inches) and then move your front foot an equal distance.

**3. Moving right (sidestep right)** - from your fighting stance, first move your right foot to the right (approximately 12 inches) and then move your left foot an equal distance.

**4. Moving left (sidestep left)** - from your fighting stance, first move your left foot to the left (approximately 12 inches) and then move your right foot an equal distance.

Practice these four movements for 10 to 15 minutes a day in front of a full-length mirror. In a couple weeks, your footwork should be quick, balanced, and natural.

*Footwork and mobility play a very important role when working out on the heavy bag.*

## Circling Right and Left

Strategic circling is an advanced form of footwork where you will use your front leg as a pivot point. This type of movement permits you to move 360-degrees around the bag and also allow you to strike from various angles. Strategic circling can be performed from either a left or right stance.

**Circling left (from a left stance)** - this means you'll be moving your body around the heavy bag in a clockwise direction. From a left stance, step 8 to 12 inches to the left with your left foot, then use your left leg as a pivot point and wheel your entire rear leg to the left until the correct stance and positioning is acquired.

**Circling right (from a right stance)** - from a right stance, step 8 to 12 inches to the right with your right foot, then use your right leg as a pivot point and wheel your entire rear leg to the right until the correct stance and positioning is acquired.

*Reality is the key! Try to visualize the heavy bag as a living breathing opponent who will hit back the moment you let your guard down.*

# Avoid Cross-Stepping When Hitting The Bag

Cross-stepping is the process of crossing one foot in front or behind the other when moving around the bag. Such sloppy footwork makes you vulnerable to a variety of problems. Some include:

- It severely compromises your balance.
- It restricts the offensive flow of punching.
- It limits quick and rapid footwork.
- It can lead to a sprained ankle.

As I said earlier, the best way to avoid cross-stepping is to follow this basic footwork rule of thumb: *Always move the foot closest to the direction you want to go first, and let the other foot follow an equal distance.*

# Explosive Footwork

Explosive footwork is another important component of heavy bag training. In fact, this type of dynamic movement plays a vital role in both offensive and defensive fighting. In offense, explosive footwork allows you to rush your target and maintain a devastating compound attack. In defense, it permits you to disengage quickly from the range of an overwhelming assault.

Explosive footwork is predicated on the following five important factors. They include the following:

1. **Basic footwork** - you must first master the basic footwork skills before incorporating ballistic movements.

2. **Proper body posture** - maintaining correct body posture through footwork movements will prevent loss of balance.

3. **Powerful legs**- strong and powerful upper and lower legs will allow you to launch your body effortlessly through the ranges of combat.

4.  **Equal weight distribution** - a noncommittal weight distribution (fifty percent on each leg) will permit you to move instantly in any direction.

5.  **Raised heel** - this creates a springlike effect in your footwork movements.

*Although there are many components of efficient footwork, moving on the balls of your feet is vital. Flat-footed footwork will slow you down considerably during your bag training.*

# Chapter 4
# How to Punch

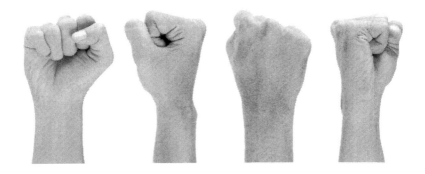

# Injury Free Punching

Since the majority of your heavy bag techniques will be delivered with your fists, it's essential that you know how to punch without sustaining a hand injury. Essentially, this requires you to understand and ultimately master a few concepts and body mechanic principles. Keep in mind that you do not have to be a professional boxer or martial arts expert to master these fundamental principles.

# What Causes Hand Injuries?

There are four main causes of punching related hand injuries. They are incorrect fist configuration, skeletal misalignment, weak hands, wrist and forearms and hitting the wrong anatomical target.

While there are different body mechanics for each and every punch, there are four things that must take place to avoid a hand injury, when hitting the heavy bag. They include the following:

- Knowing how to make a proper fist.
- Possessing strong hands, wrists, and forearms.
- Maintaining skeletal alignment when striking the bag.
- Pinpoint target accuracy.

## How to Make a Proper Fist

The first thing you need to do is learn the proper way make a fist. It's ironic that some of the most experienced fighters and martial artists don't know how to make a proper fist. As you can imagine, improper fist clenching can be disastrous for some of the following reasons:

- You can jam, sprain, or break your fingers.
- You can destroy wrist alignment, resulting in a sprained or broken wrist.

- You'll lose significant impact power when hitting the bag.

To make a proper fist, make sure your fingers are tightly clenched and that your thumb is securely wrapped around your second and third knuckles. Your fist should resemble a solid brick. Remember, if you cannot make a proper fist, you will not be capable of delivering a solid punch on the heavy bag!

*Pictured here, the correct way to make a fist.*

*Long fingernails will compromise the structural integrity of your punch by causing your individual fingers to protrude from your fist. This can easily lead to a severe hand or wrist injury. If you are serious about heavy bag training, consider keeping all of your fingernails very short.*

## You Must Keep Everything Straight

Now that you know how to make a proper fist, your next step is learning how to maintaining skeletal alignment when your fist makes contact with the bag. Skeletal alignment will help ensure that both your hand and wrists will not buckle and break during impact with the heavy bag.

*One of the biggest mistakes beginners make when making a fist is allowing their thumbs to protrude outward. This hand position is dangerous and can often lead to hand and finger injuries as well as powerless blows. Remember, always to keep your thumbs tightly wrapped around the other two fingers when throwing punches.*

## Center Knuckle Contact

In order to maintain skeletal alignment when punching, you need to learn to punch with your center knuckle first. Punching with the center of your knuckle is important because it affords proper alignment and maximizes the impact of your blow.

Excluding hammer fist strikes, every conceivable punch (i.e., jab, rear cross, hook, uppercut, shovel hook, etc) can be delivered with center knuckle contact.

Center knuckle contact also prevents a broken hand or "boxer's fracture" from occurring. Essentially, a boxer's fracture occurs when the small metacarpal bone bends downward and toward the palm of the hand during impact with an extremely hard surface (such as a brick wall or human skull).

Contrary to what karate schools teach, I suggest that you avoid striking the heavy bag with your first two knuckles. This karate style of punching diffuses the weight transfer of the punch which can easily lead to a broken hand.

## Wrist and Forearm Alignment

If you want to avoid breaking or spraining your wrists, you must always remember to keep your wrists aligned with your forearm throughout the execution of your punch. This applies to both linear punches (jab, rear cross) as well as circular punches (hooks, uppercuts and shovel hooks).

If your wrist bends or collapses on impact, you will either sprain or break it. It's that simple. Remember, a sprained or broken wrist will set back your bag training for months.

Also, don't make the false assumption that boxing gloves or hands wraps will always keep your wrists straight. I know of several fighters who actually sprained their wrists while wearing both hand wraps and boxing gloves.

*If you want to avoid breaking or spraining your wrists, you must always remember to keep your wrists aligned with your forearm throughout the execution of your punch.*

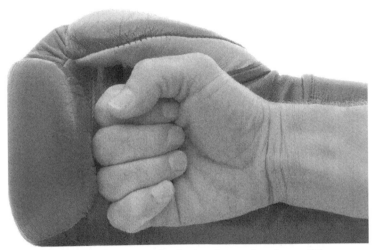

*Don't make the false assumption that boxing gloves or bag gloves will keep your wrists straight. I can assure you, they won't.*

Ironically, one of the best ways to learn how to throw a punch without bending your wrists is to regularly workout on the heavy bag. The heavy bag will provide the necessary amount of resistance to progressively strengthen and condition the bones, tendons and ligaments in your wrists. Just remember to start off slowly and gradually increase the force of your punches.

## Strong Hands, Wrists and Forearms

Proper fist configuration and wrist alignment are critical, but that is really only half of the equation. You must have strong hands, wrists, and forearms to withstand the actual force of hitting the heavy bag.

You will, therefore, need to perform specific hand and forearm exercises to strengthen these muscles. Bruce Lee was well aware of this important fact. As a matter of fact, he would religiously strengthen and develop his hands and forearms for the rigors of power punching. Lee knew that powerful and injury free punching depends largely on the overall strength and structural integrity of your hands, wrists and forearms.

# Conditioning and Strength Training

There are many efficient ways of strengthening your hands, wrists and forearms for heavy bag training. If you are low on cash and just starting out, you can begin by squeezing a tennis ball a couple times per week. One hundred repetitions per hand would be a good start.

## Power Putty

Later on you can add power putty to your hand strengthening routine. This unique hand exerciser is made up of silicone rubber that can be squeezed, pulled, pinched, clawed and stretched in just about any conceivable direction. This tough, resistant putty will strengthen the muscles of your forearm, wrists, hands and fingers.

## Hand Grippers

Another quick and effective way to strengthen your hands, wrists and forearms is to work out with heavy duty hand grippers. While there are a wide selection of them on the market, I prefer using the Captains of Crush brand. These high-quality grippers are virtually indestructible and they come in a variety of different resistance levels ranging from 60 to 365 pounds.

## Weight Training

Finally, you can condition your wrists and forearms by performing various forearm exercises with free weights. Exercises like hammer curls, reverse curls, wrist curls, and reverse wrist curls are great for developing strong wrists, forearms, and hands. When training your forearms, be sure to work both your extensor and flexor muscles. Here are a few to get you started:

### Barbell Wrist Curls

This exercise strengthens the flexor muscles. Perform 5 sets of 8-10 repetitions. To perform the exercise, follow these steps:

1. Sit at the end of a bench, grab a barbell with an underhand grip and place both of your hands close together.

2. In a smooth and controlled fashion, slowly bend your wrists and lower the barbell toward the floor.

3. Contract your forearms and curl the weight back to the starting position.

## Reverse Wrist Curls

This exercise develops and strengthens the extensor muscle of the forearm. Perform 6 sets of 6-8 repetitions. To perform the exercise, follow these steps:

1. Sit at the end of a bench, hold a barbell with an overhand grip (your hands should be approximately 11 inches apart) and place your forearms on top of your thighs.

2. Slowly lower the barbell as far as your wrists will allow.

3. Flex your wrists upward back to the starting position.

## Behind-the-Back Wrist Curls

This exercise strengthens both the flexor muscles of the forearms. Perform 5 sets of 6-8 repetitions To perform the exercise, follow these steps:

1. Hold a barbell behind your back at arm's length (your hands should be approximately shoulder-width apart).

2. Uncurl your finger and let the barbell slowly roll down your palms.

3. Close your hands and roll the barbell back into your hands.

## Hammer Curls

This exercise strengthens both the Brachialis and Brachioradialis muscles. Perform 5 sets of 8-10 repetitions. To perform the exercise, follow these steps:

1. Stand with both feet approximately shoulder-width apart, with both dumbbells at your sides.

2. Keeping your elbows close to your body and your palms facing inward, slowly curl both dumbbells upward towards your shoulders.

3. Slowly return to the starting position.

## Reverse Barbell Curls

Reverse curls can be a great alternative to hammer curls. This exercise strengthens both the Brachialis and Brachioradialis muscles. Perform 5 sets of 8-10 repetitions. To perform the exercise, follow these steps:

1. Stand with both feet approximately shoulder width apart. Hold a barbell with your palms facing down (pronated grip).

2. Keeping your upper arms stationary, curl the weights up until the bar is at shoulder level.

3. Slowly return to the starting position.

## Accuracy Counts!

The final component of injury free punching is target accuracy. For example, in a real world self-defense encounter you must avoid hitting hard body surfaces like the opponent's skull.

Believe it or not, many self-defense hand injuries are a result of striking the opponent's skull, which is extremely hard and resilient. It is likened to a crash helmet that protects the human brain from all forms of impact. I know several fighters who broke their hands when their fists connected with an opponent's forehead or skull.

Similarly, in heavy bag training, you too must be careful where you place your punches. It's important that your strikes are accurate, and your punches are timed correctly. This can be especially challenging considering that the heavy bag is always moving in unpredictable directions. Just keep in mind that one misplaced power punch can easily sprain or break your wrist.

*Since the heavy bag is constantly moving, you need to be especially careful timing the delivery of your punches.*

## Be Aware of What You Are Doing!

Learning how to punch correctly also means you will have to study and observe each and every punch in your arsenal and make certain they can handle the rigors of heavy bag work. Through proper analytical observation, you can quickly identify the strengths and weaknesses of each punch in your arsenal. The best way to accomplish this is to methodically test each punch on the heavy bag.

For example, take the most basic punch known to man - the rear cross. For those who may not be aware, the rear cross is one of the most powerful punches in a fighter's arsenal.

Begin by standing approximately four to five feet from the bag. Then, assume a fighting stance with your left leg forward and your body positioned at a forty-five degree angle from the bag. Make certain both of your hands are properly clenched into fists and your head and chin are angled slightly down.

Now, deliver the punch, exhale and quickly twist and throw your rear arm and shoulder forward and towards the heavy bag. Make certain to twist your rear leg, hip and shoulder forward and extend your rear arm straight. Do not lock out your rear arm when throwing the punch, be certain there is a slight bend in the elbow. Your punch should forcefully snap into the bag and then return to the starting position. For more information about the rear cross, see Chapter 5.

After delivering the punch to the heavy bag, make the following important observations:

- What was the overall feeling of the punch when you delivered it? Did it feel rigid and forced or was it loose and fluid?

- What happened when your punch connected with the bag? Did the punch snap or crack the heavy bag? Or did it just nudge it?

- Did anything feel strained or hurt when your fist initially connected with the bag?

- Was your punch accurate? Did you hit the bag exactly where you intended?

- Did you remember to exhale or did you hold your breath when you threw the punch?

- What happened to the structural integrity of your fist when you make contact with the punching bag? Did your fists open? Did your thumb get in the way? Did your wrist buckle inward?

- Which knuckle made initial contact with the punching bag?

You also might want to consider video taping yourself so you can quickly identify mistakes and errors in your punching form. Or perhaps you can have your training partner observe your punching technique and give you constructive feedback.

## The Punching Mitts

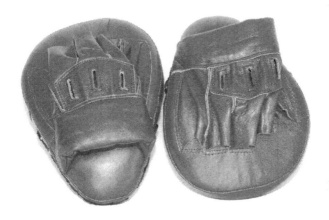

If you find the heavy bag to be a bit intimidating to work with, you can always start off with the punching mitts (also called focus mitts) to examine your punching form.

Unlike the heavy bag, the punching mitts are more forgiving on your wrists and hands and will allow you to gradually build up your power as your punching form improves.

Punching mitts will challenge even the most seasoned fighter by improving both offensive and defensive fighting skills, punching speed, stamina, rhythm, endurance, accuracy, timing, reflexes, footwork, punching combinations, punching power and counter punching techniques.

## Heavy Bag Training

The only downside to working with the punching mitts is they will require a training partner to hold them for you. The good news is, once you have trained on the mitts, you can then finally graduate to the heavy bag.

# Chapter 5
# Heavy Bag Techniques

# Fighting Ranges

Before we get into specific heavy bag techniques, you first need to understand that the distance and angle of the heavy bag will often dictate which striking technique you can execute at any given moment. Therefore, you must know about the three fighting ranges. They include: kicking, punching, and grappling range.

## Kicking Range

The furthest distance is kicking range. At this range you are usually too far away to punch the heavy bag, so you would use your legs to make contact. Kicking range techniques are powerful and can give your legs a tremendous workout.

Important: If you are strictly interested in heavy bag training for boxing, you can skip this section and focus exclusively on Section 2 of this chapter.

While there are a myriad of kicking techniques in the martial arts world, here's a list of some of the basic kicking techniques you can use on the heavy bag:

- **Push kick (front leg)**
- **Push kick (back leg)**
- **Side kick (front leg)**
- **Hook kick (front leg)**
- **Hook kick (back leg)**

*If you are going to execute kicking techniques in a real fight, always employ low-line kicks to targets below the assailant's waist. They are efficient, effective, deceptive, non-telegraphic, and relatively safe. Low-line targets include the groin, quadriceps, common peroneal nerve (approximately 4 inches above the knee area), knee, and shin.*

*Pictured here, the kicking range.*

## Push Kick (from the front leg)

1.  To perform the kick, begin from an orthodox stance (left side forward).

2.  While maintaining your balance, shift your weight onto your back leg and raise your front leg up (your front knee should be bent at approximately 90 degrees).

3.  Next, thrust with your hips and drive the ball of your front foot into the heavy bag.

4.  After contact is made with the bag, quickly retract your leg to the starting position. Remember to always keep your hands up when performing kicking techniques.

*When performing the push kick on the heavy bag, be certain to make contact with the ball of your foot and not your toes. Striking the bag with your toes can easily lead to a severe injury.*

*Here, the fighter delivers a push kick from his front leg.*

## Push Kick (from the rear leg)

1. To perform the kick, begin from an orthodox stance (left side forward).

2. While maintaining your balance, push your back foot off the ground and shift your weight to your front leg (your rear knee should be bent at approximately 90 degrees).

3. Next, thrust with your hips and drive the ball of your foot

into the heavy bag.

4. After contact is made with the bag, quickly retract your leg to the starting position. Again, make certain to make contact with the ball of your foot and not your toes.

## Side Kick (from the front leg)

1. The side kick is a powerful linear kick executed from the lead leg. Contact is made with the heel of your foot. To perform the kick, begin from an orthodox stance (left side facing the heavy bag).

2. While maintaining your balance, lean back and shift your weight onto your rear leg while simultaneously pivoting your body so your centerline is approximately 90 degrees from the bag.

3. Raise your front knee up and close to your body (this is called the "chamber" position).

4. Next, use your hips and thrust your front leg forcefully into the bag. Contact is made with the heel of your foot.

5. After contact is made with the heavy bag, retract your leg to the starting position.

*Here are two common mistakes that occur when executing a side kick: (1) Failure to chamber your leg - your kick will have no force. To remedy this, lift your leg to the bent-knee position (this is known as a moderate chamber position). (2) Your toes lead the extension - you will jam your toes and sprain your ankle. To remedy this, pull your toes back toward your knee. This will ensure that your kick is leading with the heel of your foot.*

*While kicking above the waist is not recommended for street combat, you can still add them to your heavy bag workouts.*

*One of the most important considerations when executing a side kick is maintaining proper skeletal alignment. Skeletal alignment is the proper alignment or arrangement of your body, which maximizes the structural integrity of your striking limb. Therefore, when executing a side kick, always make certain that the heel, knee, and hip of your kicking leg are properly aligned.*

# Hook kick (front leg)

1. To perform the hook kick from your front leg, begin from an orthodox stance (left side facing the heavy bag).

2. While maintaining your balance, lean back slightly and shift your weight to your rear leg.

3. Simultaneously raise your front knee up and towards the bag.

4. Next, quickly twist your front hip and swing your lead leg forcefully into the bag. Your front knee should be slightly bent when impact is made with the target. Avoid snapping your knee when performing the kick. Contact should be made with either the dorsum of your foot or shin bone.

5. After contact is made with the heavy bag, bring your leg back to the starting position.

*In this photo, the fighter performs a hook kick with his front leg.*

## Hook kick (rear leg)

1.  To perform the hook kick from your rear leg, begin from an orthodox stance (left side facing the heavy bag).

2.  While maintaining your balance, push off the back foot and shift your weight forward.

3.  Next, raise your rear knee up and twist your hips forward as you swing your rear leg forcefully into the bag.

4.  Your rear knee should be slightly bent when impact is made with the bag. Avoid snapping your knee when performing the hook kick. Once again, contact should be made with either the dorsum of your foot or shin bone.

5.  After contact is made with the bag, bring your leg back to the starting position.

*The hook kick is also a devastating self-defense technique that can collapse and temporarily immobilize the assailant's leg. Keep in mind that if you strike the assailant's knee you can cause permanent damage to the cartilage, ligaments, tendons and bones.*

*While the traditional round house kick might look similar to the hook kick, it differs significantly. Round house kicks are generally snapping kicks generated from the knee, while hook kicks are driving kicks that generate tremendous power from the hips. Pictured here, a woman performs a traditional round house kick on the heavy bag.*

*Heavy bag training is not limited to any particular style of fighting. Here, a traditional martial artist performs a groin kick on the bag.*

*When performing kicking technique on the heavy bag, try to avoid remaining stationary. Get into the habit of constantly moving around the heavy bag with quick and economical steps.*

# Punching Range

The next distance of fighting is punching range and it's the mid-range of combat. At this distance, you are close enough to the bag to strike it with your fists. Punching range techniques should be quick and efficient and they should be the foundation of your heavy bag arsenal.

For those of you who are interested in reality based self-defense training, I strongly encourage you to specialize in the punching range. Here are just a few reasons why:

- The opponent's defensive reaction time is reduced in punching range.

- Unlike kicking techniques, you can efficiently neutralize your adversary with punches and other hand strikes.

- Compared to the other ranges of unarmed combat, punching range techniques are more efficient - there is less energy expenditure.

- Punching range techniques are less telegraphic than kicking range tools.

- Compared to grappling range (vertical & horizontal planes), punching range only requires moderate bodily commitment.

- Unlike kicking range, there is less "space requirement" necessary to deploy most of your punching range techniques.

- Unlike grappling range combat, there is virtually no bodily entanglement, so multiple assailants can be fought in the punching range of unarmed combat.

## Punching Techniques and Western Boxing

Punching range is the midrange of unarmed fighting. At this distance, you are close enough to the heavy bag to strike with your hands fists. Interestingly enough, amateur and professional boxers focus exclusively on this range of unarmed combat.

Here's a list of some of the punching techniques that you can perform on the heavy bag.

- Jab
- **Rear cross (also called the straight right)**
- **Hook punch**
- **Uppercut punch**

*The punching range.*

*Very little has changed since the golden age of boxing. Amateur and professional boxers alike focus exclusively on punching techniques for their sport.*

## The Jab

The jab is a foundation technique for boxers and mixed martial artists. This punch is thrown from your front hand and it has a quick snap when delivered.

1. Start off in a fighting stance with both of your hands held up in the guard position. Your fists should be lightly clenched with both of your elbows pointing to the ground.

2. To perform the punch, simultaneously step toward the bag and twist your front waist and shoulder forward as you snap your front arm into the bag.

3. When delivering the punch, remember not to lock out your arm as this will have a "pushing effect" on the heavy bag.

4. Quickly retract your arm back to the starting position.

One common mistake when throwing the jab is to let it deflect off to the side of the bag. Also, keep in mind that jabs can be delivered to the head (top of the heavy bag) or the body (middle of the bag).

*When executing linear punches (i.e. jabs, rear crosses,etc) on the heavy bag, remember that your line of initiation should always be your line of retraction. Avoid arcing or dropping your blow after contact is made with the bag. Such sloppy body mechanics will throw you off balance and diminish your impact power.*

*In boxing and mixed martial arts, the jab is an essential punch used to throw the opponent off balance, set him up for other blows, test his reflexes, and keep him from moving toward you.*

# Using the Jab for Street Self-Defense

While the jab might be appropriate for boxing, mixed martial arts and other forms of combat sport competition, it has no purpose in real world combat. The truth is the jab is combatively deficient for some of the following reasons:

- It lacks neutralizing power.

- It can expose you to a counter attack.

- It often agitates the assailant more than it harms him.

- It prolongs a self defense altercation and allows the assailant the opportunity to escalate his level of force against you.

- It's a probing and point scoring tool.

If self-defense is your interest and concern, you can simply replace the Jab with the Lead Straight punch. Like the jab, the lead straight is also a linear punch thrown from your lead arm, however this punch is much more powerful and can be used on the heavy bag as well as real life self-defense situations.

*The lead straight is a linear punch thrown from your lead arm and contact is made with the center knuckle. To execute the lead straight, quickly twist your lead leg, hip, and shoulder forward. Snap your blow into the assailant's target and return back to the starting position. A common mistake is to throw the punch and let it deflect off to the side of the heavy bag.*

# Rear Cross

The rear cross (also called the straight right) is considered the heavy artillery of punches and it's thrown from your rear arm. To execute the punch, perform the following steps:

1. Start off in a fighting stance with both of your hands held up in the guard position. Your fists should be lightly clenched with both of your elbows pointing to the ground.

2. To perform the punch, quickly twist your rear hips and shoulders forward as you snap your rear arm into the heavy bag. Proper waist twisting and weight transfer is of paramount importance to the rear cross. You must shift your weight from your rear foot to your lead leg as you throw the punch.

3. To maximize the impact of the punch, make certain that your fist is positioned horizontally. Avoid overextending the blow or exposing your chin during its execution.

4. Once again, do not lock out your arm when throwing the punch. Let the power of the punch sink into the bag before you retract it back to the starting position.

*The rear cross is an extremely powerful punch that can be delivered to both high and low targets on the heavy bag.*

When throwing the rear cross, be certain not to lock your elbow. Elbow locking is a common problem among novices. There should always be a slight bend in your elbow when the punch hits the bag. Remember, if your elbow locks upon impact, it will have a "pushing effect" and rob you of critical knock-out power.

Another common mistake when throwing the rear cross on the bag is to let the punch glide downwards after contact is made. Always remember, the trajectory of initiating your punch must also be the very same trajectory of retracting your punch.

*When delivering the rear cross, remember to turn your palm down so your fists hit the bag horizontally.*

*Remember to completely tighten your fists when impact is made with the heavy bag. This action will allow your natural body weapon to travel with optimum speed and efficiency, and it will also augment the impact power of your punch.*

## Hook Punch

The hook is another devastating punch in your arsenal of techniques, yet it's also one of the most difficult to master. This punch can be performed from either your front or rear hand and it can be thrown high or low to the heavy bag. There are actually two variations of the hook punch, they include:

- **Traditional Hook Punch**

- **Modified Hook Punch**

For the purposes of this book, I will teach you the traditional hook punch that is used in most boxing circles. Once again, if you would like to learn about the modified hook punch, which is used exclusively for street self-defense applications, you might want to look into my other books for more information.

1. Start in a fighting stance with your hand guard held up.

2. To execute the hook punch, quickly and smoothly, raise your elbow up so that your arm is parallel to the ground while simultaneously torquing your shoulder, hip, and foot into the

direction of the blow.

3.  When delivering the strike, be certain your arm is bent at least ninety degrees and that your wrist and forearm are kept straight throughout the movement.

4.  As you throw the punch, your fist is positioned horizontally. The elbow should be locked when contact is made with the heavy bag.

5.  Return back to the starting position.

*When delivering the hook punch, remember to maintain the proper wrist, forearm and shoulder alignment at all times.*

*The hook is one of the most devastating blows in your arsenal. However, it's also one of the most difficult to master. To properly execute the hook punch, you must maintain the proper wrist, forearm, and shoulder alignment. When delivering the strike, be certain your arm is bent at least ninety degrees and that your wrist and forearm are kept straight throughout the entire movement.*

*The modified hook punch is specifically suited for reality based self-defense applications. In this photo, notice how the practitioner's fist is positioned vertically.*

## Uppercut Punch

The uppercut is a another powerful punch that can be delivered from both the lead and rear arm. Due to its unusual angle of delivery, the uppercut is best practiced on either the punching mitts or uppercut bag. However, with a bit of careful practice it can be practiced on the heavy bag.

1.  Start off in a fighting stance with both of your hands held up in the guard position. Your fists should be lightly clenched with both of your elbows pointing to the ground.

2.  To execute the uppercut, drop your shoulder and bend your knees.

3.  Quickly, stand up and drive your fist upward and into the heavy bag. Your palm should be facing you when contact is made with the heavy bag. To avoid any possible injury, keep your wrists straight.

4.  Make certain that the punch has a tight arc and that you avoid any and all "winding up" motions. A properly executed uppercut should be a tight punch and should feel like an explosive jolt.

5.  Return back to the fighting stance.

*The real key to delivering a powerful uppercut punch is the lifting of your legs into the direction of your blow.*

*Pictured here, the rear uppercut punch.*

*In the early 1800's, the famous boxer pioneer, Samuel Elias (also known as Dutch Sam), was responsible for discovering the right hand "undercut" which was later called the uppercut.*

*There are two major problems with the uppercut featured in this photo. First, the practitioner is too far from the heavy bag. Second, he's curling his wrists which can easily lead to a sprain or break.*

*When performing the uppercut, avoid any and all wind up motions. This is what you should not do!*

*While the uppercut punch is best suited for the punching mitts, it can also be practiced on the heavy bag. Just remember to keep your wrists straight when making contact with the bag.*

# Grappling Range

The third and closest range of fighting is grappling range. At this distance, you are too close to the bag to kick or execute linear punches, so you would use close-quarter strikes.

Grappling range is actually divided into two different planes; vertical and horizontal. In the vertical plane, you would deliver impact techniques, some of which include elbow and knee strikes, head butts, gouging and crushing tactics, and biting and tearing techniques.

In the horizontal plane of grappling range, you are ground fighting with your opponent and can deliver all of the previously mentioned techniques, including various submission holds, locks and chokes.

When it comes to heavy bag training, grappling range striking techniques are going to appeal to three groups of people:

- **Self-defense practitioners**
- **Mixed martial artists (MMA)**
- **Martial artists (traditional and eclectics)**

You can add a couple grappling range strikes to your heavy bag workouts. Here are two:

- **Elbow strikes**
- **Knee strikes**

*Combining offensive strikes from all three ranges of fighting (kicking, punching and grappling) during your heavy bag workouts will thoroughly condition your body from head to toe.*

*The Grappling range.*

## Horizontal Elbow

The elbows are devastating weapons that can be used in the grappling range. They are explosive, deceptive and very difficult to stop. Elbows can generally be delivered horizontally, vertically, diagonally and they can be thrown from either your front or rear arm.

Let's just take a look at the body mechanics of the horizontal elbow strike

1.  Start off in a fighting stance with both of your hands held up in the guard position. Make certain that you are standing in close proximity to the heavy bag.

2.  To execute the elbow strike, quickly and smoothly, raise your elbow up so that your arm is parallel to the ground.

3. Next, simultaneously torquing your shoulder, hip, and foot into the direction of the bag. The tip of your elbow should make contact with the target.

4. Return back to the starting position.

*Pictured here, a horizontal elbow strike delivered from the rear arm.*

*Be careful when delivering elbow strikes on a canvas heavy bag. The material can quickly tear up the skin on your elbows, leaving your bag permanently strained with blood.*

## Diagonal Knee Strike

The knee strike is another devastating close-quarter grappling range tool that can do a lot of damage. The knee strike can also be delivered diagonally or vertically to the heavy bag.

Here are the body mechanics of the diagonal knee strike.

1.  To perform the diagonal knee strike from your rear leg, begin from an orthodox stance (left side facing the heavy bag).

2.  Next, grab hold of the bag with both hands.

3.  While maintaining your balance, push off the back foot and shift your weight forward.

4.  Next, raise your rear knee up and swing your hips and rear leg diagonally into the bag.

5.  Your rear knee should be sharply bent when impact is made with the bag.

6.  After contact is made, bring your leg back to the starting position.

*When delivering knee strikes, keep your rear leg bent with your toe pointed to the ground. This toe position helps maintain proper skeletal alignment; protects your toes from unnecessary injury; and facilitates quick and rapid delivery.*

*The diagonal knee strike.*

## Vertical Knee Strike

1. To perform the vertical knee strike from your rear leg, begin from an orthodox stance (left side facing the heavy bag).

2. Next, grab hold of the bag with both hands.

3. While maintaining your balance, push off the back foot and shift your weight forward.

4. Next, raise your rear knee up and drive your hips and rear leg vertically into the heavy bag.

5. Your rear knee should be sharply bent when impact is made with the bag.

6. After contact is made with the bag, bring your leg back to the starting position.

# Heavy Bag Training

# Chapter 6
# Heavy Bag Workouts

# Three Heavy Bag Training Methods

Over the past thirty years of teaching the martial arts, I have developed three unique training methodologies that can be applied to heavy bag training. They include Proficiency, Conditioning and Street Training. Let's take a look at each one.

## Conditioning Training

Conditioning Training is primarily used by boxers, mixed martial artists, kickboxers, self-defense technicians and fitness enthusiasts who wish to train on the heavy bag for specified period of time called "rounds". Depending on the practitioner's level of conditioning, each round can range anywhere from one to five minutes. Each round is then separated by either 30-second, one-minute or two-minute breaks. A good heavy bag workout consists of at least five to eight rounds.

Conditioning Training is performed at a moderate pace, and it develops cardiovascular fitness, muscular endurance, fluidity, rhythm, distancing, timing, speed, footwork, and balance. Many fitness enthusiasts looking to burn fat will use this methodology as it tends to burn a significant amount of calories.

Conditioning Training does require that you have a fundamental understanding of piecing punches and kicks together into logical combinations.

## Proficiency Training

The second training methodology is Proficiency Training and it's generally used by martial artists and self-defense practitioners who want to sharpen one specific punch, kick, or strike at a time by executing it over and over for a prescribed number of repetitions. Each time the technique is performed with "clean" form at various speeds. Punches are also performed with the eyes closed to develop a kinesthetic "feel" for the action.

Proficiency Training on the heavy bag develops speed, power, accuracy, non-telegraphic movement, balance, and general psychomotor skill.

## Street Training

The third and final training methodology is Street Training, and it's specially designed for reality-based self-defense preparation.

Since most self-defense altercations are explosive, lasting an average of 20 seconds, the practitioner must prepare for this possible scenario. This means delivering explosive and powerful compound attacks with vicious intent for approximately 20 seconds, resting one minute, and then repeating the process.

Street Training prepares you for the stress and immediate fatigue of a real fight. It also develops speed, power, explosiveness, target selection and recognition, timing, footwork and breath control.

# Designing Your Heavy Bag Workout

While all three training methodologies are important, we are going to focus exclusively on Conditioning Training, which means we are going to focus on "time based" workouts.

## Time Based Workouts

Essentially, a time based heavy bag workout is based on "rounds" and it's an ideal way to structure your workouts. Before you begin, now is the time to decide on the duration of your rounds as well as the rest intervals.

## Heavy Bag Training

In most cases, mixed martial artists, boxers and kick boxers will work the heavy bag for three-minute rounds with one-minute rest periods. Depending on their level of conditioning and specific training goals, they might do this for a total of 5 to 8 rounds.

Initially, you'll need to experiment with both the round duration and rest intervals to see what works best for you. Remember to start off slow and progressively build up the intensity and duration of your workouts. Remember to work with the bag and not try to kill it!

To get you started, here are some sample time-based workouts you might want to try. Keep in mind, the Advanced Level workouts

| Sample Time Based Heavy Bag Workouts | | | |
|---|---|---|---|
| Skill Level | Duration of Each Round | Rest Period | Total Number of rounds |
| Beginner | 1 minute | 2 minutes | 3 |
| Beginner | 1 minute | 1 minute | 3 |
| Beginner | 2 minutes | 2 minute | 3 |
| Beginner | 2 minutes | 1 minute | 3 |
| Intermediate | 3 minutes | 2 minutes | 5 |
| Intermediate | 3 minutes | 1 minute | 5 |
| Intermediate | 3 minutes | 2 minute | 6 |
| Intermediate | 3 minutes | 1 minute | 6 |
| Advanced | 4 minutes | 2 minutes | 8 |
| Advanced | 4 minutes | 1 minute | 8 |
| Advanced | 5 minutes | 2 minutes | 10 |
| Advanced | 5 minutes | 1 minute | 10 |

are for elite fighters who have a minimum of 5 years of heavy bag training and conditioning.

## A Word of Caution!

Take your time when working out on the bag. If you are learning how to use the heavy bag for the very first time, I strongly urge you to take your time and develop the proper punching and kicking body mechanics before tearing into the bag.

Remember, the heavy bag is a serious piece of training equipment, and it is easy to get injured when using it. Heavy bag workouts are also tough and very demanding. Avoid premature exhaustion by pacing yourself during your workouts. Remember, it's not a race! Enjoy the process of learning how to use the bag with skill and finesse.

Warning! Before you begin any exercise program, including those suggested in this book, it is important to check with your doctor to see if you have any condition that might be aggravated by strenuous exercise.

## What is a Combination?

A combination or "compound attack" is the logical sequence of two or more techniques thrown in strategic succession. For example, a jab followed immediately by a rear cross is considered to be a punching combination.

There are an infinite amount of fighting combinations you can perform on the heavy bag. Frankly, you are only limited by your own imagination.

When reading the combination sequence, please note that the word "high" indicates punches delivered at head level on the heavy bag and the word "low" indicates punches delivered at the stomach level on the bag.

## Punching Combinations

What follows are just a few punching combinations you can employ in your heavy bag workouts. If you require advanced heavy bag combination training, including step-by-step photographs, please see my book, *Heavy Bag Combinations: The Ultimate Guide to Heavy Bag Punching Combinations*.

- Jab (high) - Jab (high)
- Jab (low) - Jab (low)
- Jab (high) - Jab (low)
- Jab (low) - Jab (high)
- Jab (high) - Jab (high) - Rear Cross (high)
- Jab (high) - Jab (high) - Rear Cross (low)
- Jab - Rear Cross (high)
- Jab - Rear Cross (low)
- Jab - Rear Cross (high) - Jab
- Jab - Rear Cross (low) - Jab
- Jab - Rear Cross - Jab - Rear Cross
- Jab - Jab - Rear Cross
- Jab - Rear Cross - Jab
- Jab - Rear Cross - Lead Hook (high)
- Jab - Rear Cross - Lead Hook (low)
- Jab - Rear Cross - Lead Hook (high) - Rear Hook (high)
- Jab - Rear Cross - Lead Hook (low) - Rear Hook (low)
- Jab - Rear Cross - Lead Hook (high) - Rear Hook (low)

## Heavy Bag Training

- Jab - Rear Cross - Lead Hook (low) - Rear Hook (high)

- Jab - Rear Hook (high)

- Jab - Rear Hook (low)

- Jab - Lead Hook (high)

- Jab - Lead Hook (low)

- Jab - Lead Hook (high) - Rear hook (high)

- Jab - Lead Hook (low) - Rear hook (low)

- Jab - Lead Hook (high) - Rear hook (low)

- Jab - Lead Hook (low) - Rear hook (high)

- Jab - Jab - Rear Cross - Lead Hook (high)

- Jab - Jab - Rear Cross - Lead Hook (low)

- Jab - Rear Cross - Lead Hook (high) - Rear Uppercut

- Jab - Rear Cross - Lead Hook (high) - Rear Hook (low) - Lead Uppercut

- Rear Cross - Horizontal Elbow (front)

- Rear Cross - Horizontal Elbow (front) - Horizontal Elbow (rear)

- Rear Cross - Horizontal Elbow (front) - Horizontal Elbow (rear) - Diagonal Knee (front)

- Rear Uppercut - Lead Hook (high)

- Rear Uppercut - Lead Hook (low)

- Rear Uppercut - Lead Hook (high) - Rear Hook (high)

- Rear Uppercut - Lead Hook (low) - Rear Hook (low)

- Rear Uppercut - Lead Hook (high) - Rear Hook (low)

*Always keep your hands up when throwing combinations on the heavy bag. Notice how the practitioner in this photo delivers a solid jab while keeping his rear hand up.*

## Kicking and Punching Combinations

Here are some kicking and punching combinations you can add to your heavy bag workouts:

- Jab - Hook Kick (rear leg)
- Jab - Jab - Hook Kick (rear leg)
- Jab - Rear Cross - Hook Kick (front leg)
- Jab - Rear Cross - Hook Kick (front leg) - Hook Kick (rear)
- Jab - Diagonal Knee (rear)
- Jab - Diagonal Knee (rear) - Diagonal Knee (front)
- Jab - Diagonal Knee (rear) - Horizontal elbow (front)
- Jab - Rear Cross - Diagonal Knee (front)
- Jab - Rear Cross - Push Kick (rear)
- Jab - Rear Cross - Jab - Rear Cross - Hook Kick (rear)
- Jab - Rear Cross - Jab - Rear Cross - Push Kick (rear)
- Jab - Rear Cross - Push Kick (rear) - Diagonal Knee (front)
- Jab - Rear Cross - Push Kick (rear) - Hook Kick (front)
- Jab - Rear Cross - Diagonal Knee (front) - Horizontal Elbow (rear)
- Push Kick (front leg) - Rear Cross (high)
- Push Kick (front leg) - Rear Cross (low)
- Push Kick (front leg) - Rear Cross (high) - Lead Hook (high)
- Push Kick (front leg) - Rear Cross (low) - Lead Hook (low)
- Push Kick (front leg) - Rear Cross (low) - Lead Hook (high)
- Push Kick (front leg) - Rear Cross (high) - Lead Hook (low)
- Push Kick (front leg) - Rear Cross (high) - Lead Hook (high) - Rear Hook (high)

*Since most women have small hands and wrists, they need to be especially careful when punching the bag. Proper hand protection is vital!*

## Heavy Bag Training

- Push Kick (front leg) - Rear Cross (high) - Lead Hook (low) - Rear Hook (low)
- Push Kick (front leg) - Rear Uppercut
- Push Kick (front leg) - Rear Uppercut - Lead Uppercut
- Push Kick (front leg) - Rear Uppercut - Lead Uppercut - Diagonal Knee (rear)
- Hook Kick (front) - Rear Cross (high)
- Hook Kick (front) - Rear Cross (low)
- Hook Kick (front) - Rear Cross (high) - Lead Hook (high)
- Hook Kick (front) - Rear Cross (high) - Lead Hook (low)
- Hook Kick (front) - Rear Hook (high) - Rear Hook (high)
- Hook Kick (front) - Rear Hook (low) - Rear Hook (low)
- Hook Kick (front) - Rear Hook (high) - Rear Hook (low)
- Hook Kick (front) - Rear Hook (low) - Rear Hook (high)
- Side Kick (front) - Jab - Rear Cross
- Side Kick (front) - Jab - Rear Cross - Lead Hook
- Side Kick (front) - Rear Cross
- Side Kick (front) - Rear Cross - Lead Straight
- Side Kick (front) - Rear Cross - Horizontal Elbow (front)
- Side Kick (front) - Rear Cross - Horizontal Elbow (front) - Horizontal Elbow (rear)
- Side Kick (front) - Rear Cross - Hook Kick (front)
- Side Kick (front) - Diagonal Knee (rear)
- Side Kick (front) - Diagonal Knee (rear) - Horizontal Elbow (front)

*Avoid hitting canvas heavy bags bare handed. They will lacerate your fingers and knuckles and permanently stain your heavy bag with blood.*

## Create Your Own Combinations

Use this section to write down your own heavy bag combinations.

1.

2.

3.

4.

5.

6.

7.

8.

9.

10.

11.

12.

13.

14.

15.

16.

17.

18.

19.

20.

21.

22.

23.

24.

25.

26.

27.

28.

29.

30.

31.

32.

33.

34.

35.

36.

37.

38.

39.

40.

# More Heavy Bag Workout Tips

- Before you begin a heavy bag program, make certain that you have been cleared by your doctor. Since there is always some risk involved in training and because each person is unique, it is important that before beginning any type of training program, you should have a complete physical examination by your physician.

- Before hitting the heavy bag, always warm up with some light stretching and calisthenics.

- Always start your first round on the heavy bag with light punches and kicks. Never go all out in the beginning of your workout session.

- When hitting the bag, never sacrifice proper technique for power or speed.

- Always throw your punching or kicking techniques from a good fighting stance.

- Don't chew gum when working out on the bag.

- Avoid wearing watches and jewelry when training.

- Consider shadow boxing with light dumbbells to strengthen your arm and shoulders for heavy bag work.

- Never hold your breath. Remember to exhale with the delivery of each and every technique.

- Before you invest your time and money in a heavy bag program, it's important to first define your goals. What do you hope to accomplish by training on the bag? For example, do you want to get in better shape? Build up your confidence? Handle a vicious street thug? Enter a mixed martial arts competition?

*If you have a training partner, he can lend some assistance by holding the heavy bag while you strike it. This can be particularly helpful because your partner can give you "real time" feedback while you are training.*

- Be cognizant of your distance from the bag at all times. Stand too close when punching the bag will result in a "pushing effect" while standing too far will just cause the blow to simply glance the target.

- When working out alone, avoid the urge to stop the bag from moving. Let it swing freely!

- Avoid the habit of tapping your gloves together before delivering a punch on the bag.

- If you don't know the proper way to throw a punch or kick, get instruction from a qualified coach or instructor.

- Avoid locking out your elbows when punching the bag.

- Be mobile when working out on the bag, avoid stationary punching.

*Avoid pulling your free hand back when throwing a punch. Instead, keep your free hand tight and close to your face when punching. In this photo, the practitioner demonstrates a common mistake beginners make when hitting the heavy bag.*

- Avoid premature exhaustion by pacing yourself during your heavy bag workouts.

- Heavy bags don't hit back, so be aware of your own target openings and vulnerabilities when hitting the bag.

- Never let children play or swing from a heavy bag.

- Remember to maintain your balance at all times when punching the bag - never sacrifice your balance for power.

*Bare knuckle training should only be performed by experienced practitioners.*

- Heavy bags are unforgiving on your body and will certainly test the structural integrity of you punches and blows. Please remember to keep your wrists straight when your fists hit the bag. Learn to gradually build up the force of your blows - a beginner's wrists are usually too weak to accommodate full force strikes on the punching bag.

- When using the heavy bag learn to relax and avoid unnecessarily tensing your arm and shoulder muscles.

Muscular tension will throw off the timing of your punches, retard the speed of your blows, kicks and strikes and most certainly wear you out during your heavy bag workout.

- Heavy bags often cause fighters to "lose their form" when delivering their blows. Try to be constantly aware of your form when hitting the bag or better yet have a training partner, teacher or coach observe you when working out on the bag. Another suggestion is to video tape yourself using the punching bag. This will give you a good idea of what you are doing in your workouts.

- Avoid heavy bag training two days in a row. Give your body a few days to recover from your last workout.

*When working out alone, avoid the tendency to stop the heavy bag from swinging. Remember, one of the advantages of heavy bag training is to learn to throw combinations at a moving target.*

# Heavy Bag Training

- To avoid injury or "burn out", don't engage in heavy bag training more than three times per week.

- Get into the habit of regularly inspecting your heavy bag for tears and other signs of wear.

- Avoid the latest gimmicks - Every so often, some cleaver marketing company will come up with a trendy gimmick that can be added to your heavy bag workouts. Keep your workouts pure and simple. Beginners should avoid adding hand weights, weighted bag gloves, resistance bands and elevations masks to their workouts.

- While most people use the heavy bag for boxing, kickboxing and mixed martial arts training, don't forget the punching bag is a fantastic tool for developing effective self-defense techniques.

- Remember that heavy bag training for combat sports is much different than heavy bag training for real world self-defense scenarios.

- Unless you are highly skilled martial artist, do not kick a heavy bag while bare foot.

- Stay hydrated when working out on the bag. Dehydration can have a real negative effect on your workout, and it can also be dangerous. When working out, always drink plenty of water. Always hydrate before your workout by drinking at least one pint of water. During the summer months, drink more water than usual. Also get into the habit of taking a water bottle with you to your workouts.

- When purchasing heavy bag gear, spare no expense. Heavy bag training is a serious matter, and your training gear should reflect it. Good equipment will provide years of reliable use and enhance your fighting skills.

*If you want to avoid a serious hand injury, be precise when hitting the heavy bag.*
*Take your time when training and progressively build up your power.*

## Heavy Bag Training

- Consider working out with music. Actually, your heavy bag workouts can be dramatically enhanced by training to music. It's my experience that training to fast, rhythmic music works wonders for conditioning training, while hard-driving aggressive rock music works best for proficiency and street training methods.

# NOTES

_____

_____

_____

_____

_____

_____

_____

_____

_____

_____

_____

_____

_____

_____

_____

_____

# Heavy Bag Resources

## Heavy Bag Videos

If you wish to explore additional information about heavy bag training, I encourage you to check out the following video and book resources. Instructional videos include the following:

- *Heavy Bag Training*
- *Punching Bag Combinations*

Both videos are available for purchase on my website and amazon.com

Heavy Bag Training DVD

Punching Bag Combinations DVD

## Heavy Bag Books

You can also find the entire Heavy Bag Training Series at Amazon.com. They are available in both paperback and kindle editions.

*Heavy Bag Combinations*
*Book #2*

*Heavy Bag Routines*
*Book #3*

# Glossary

## A

accuracy—The precise or exact projection of force. Accuracy is also defined as the ability to execute a combative movement with precision and exactness.

adaptability—The ability to physically and psychologically adjust to new or different conditions or circumstances of combat.

advanced first-strike tools—Offensive techniques that are specifically used when confronted with multiple opponents.

aerobic exercise—Literally, "with air." Exercise that elevates the heart rate to a training level for a prolonged period of time, usually 30 minutes.

affective preparedness – One of the three components of preparedness. Affective preparedness means being emotionally, philosophically, and spiritually prepared for the strains of combat. See cognitive preparedness and psychomotor preparedness.

aggression—Hostile and injurious behavior directed toward a person.

aggressive response—One of the three possible counters when assaulted by a grab, choke, or hold from a standing position. Aggressive response requires you to counter the enemy with destructive blows and strikes. See moderate response and passive response.

aggressive hand positioning—Placement of hands so as to imply aggressive or hostile intentions.

agility—An attribute of combat. One's ability to move his or her body quickly and gracefully.

amalgamation—A scientific process of uniting or merging.

ambidextrous—The ability to perform with equal facility on both the right and left sides of the body.

anabolic steroids – synthetic chemical compounds that resemble the male sex hormone testosterone. This performance-enhancing drug is known to increase lean muscle mass, strength, and endurance.

analysis and integration—One of the five elements of CFA's mental component. This is the painstaking process of breaking down various elements, concepts, sciences, and disciplines into their atomic parts, and then methodically and strategically analyzing, experimenting, and drastically modifying the information so that it fulfills three combative requirements: efficiency, effectiveness, and safety. Only then is it finally integrated into the CFA system.

anatomical striking targets—The various anatomical body targets that can be struck and which are especially vulnerable to potential harm. They include: the eyes, temple, nose, chin, back of neck, front of neck, solar plexus, ribs, groin, thighs, knees, shins, and instep.

anchoring – The strategic process of trapping the assailant's neck or limb in order to control the range of engagement during razing.

assailant—A person who threatens or attacks another person.

assault—The threat or willful attempt to inflict injury upon the person of another.

assault and battery—The unlawful touching of another person without justification.

assessment—The process of rapidly gathering, analyzing, and accurately evaluating information in terms of threat and danger. You can assess people, places, actions, and objects.

attack—Offensive action designed to physically control, injure, or kill another person.

attitude—One of the three factors that determine who wins a street fight. Attitude means being emotionally, philosophically, and spiritually liberated from societal and religious mores. See skills and knowledge.

attributes of combat—The physical, mental, and spiritual qualities that enhance combat skills and tactics.

awareness—Perception or knowledge of people, places, actions, and objects. (In CFA, there are three categories of tactical awareness: criminal awareness, situational awareness, and self-awareness.)

# B

balance—One's ability to maintain equilibrium while stationary or moving.

blading the body—Strategically positioning your body at a 45-degree angle.

blitz and disengage—A style of sparring whereby a fighter moves into a range of combat, unleashes a strategic compound attack, and then quickly disengages to a safe distance. Of all sparring methodologies, the blitz and disengage most closely resembles a real street fight.

block—A defensive tool designed to intercept the assailant's attack by placing a non-vital target between the assailant's strike and your vital body target.

body composition—The ratio of fat to lean body tissue.

body language—Nonverbal communication through posture, gestures, and facial expressions.

body mechanics—Technically precise body movement during the execution of a body weapon, defensive technique, or other fighting maneuver.

body tackle – A tackle that occurs when your opponent haphazardly rushes forward and plows his body into yours.

body weapon—Also known as a tool, one of the various body parts that can be used to strike or otherwise injure or kill a criminal assailant.

burn out—A negative emotional state acquired by physically over- training. Some symptoms include: illness, boredom, anxiety, disinterest in training, and general sluggishness.

# C

cadence—Coordinating tempo and rhythm to establish a timing pattern of movement.

cardiorespiratory conditioning—The component of physical fitness that deals with the heart, lungs, and circulatory system.

centerline—An imaginary vertical line that divides your body in half and which contains many of your vital anatomical targets.

choke holds—Holds that impair the flow of blood or oxygen to the brain.

circular movements—Movements that follow the direction of a curve.

close-quarter combat—One of the three ranges of knife and bludgeon combat. At this distance, you can strike, slash, or stab your assailant with a variety of close-quarter techniques.

cognitive development—One of the five elements of CFA's mental component. The process of developing and enhancing your fighting skills through specific mental exercises and techniques. See analysis and integration, killer instinct, philosophy, and strategic/tactical development.

cognitive exercises—Various mental exercises used to enhance fighting skills and tactics.

cognitive preparedness – One of the three components of preparedness. Cognitive preparedness means being equipped with the strategic concepts, principles, and general knowledge of combat. See affective preparedness and psychomotor preparedness.

combat-oriented training—Training that is specifically related to the harsh realities of both armed and unarmed combat. See ritual-oriented training and sport-oriented training.

combative arts—The various arts of war. See martial arts.

combative attributes—See attributes of combat.

combative fitness—A state characterized by cardiorespiratory and muscular/skeletal conditioning, as well as proper body composition.

combative mentality—Also known as the killer instinct, this is a combative state of mind necessary for fighting. See killer instinct.

combat ranges—The various ranges of unarmed combat.

combative utility—The quality of condition of being combatively useful.

combination(s)—See compound attack.

common peroneal nerve—A pressure point area located approximately four to six inches above the knee on the midline of the outside of the thigh.

composure—A combative attribute. Composure is a quiet and focused mind-set that enables you to acquire your combative agenda.

compound attack—One of the five conventional methods of attack. Two or more body weapons launched in strategic succession whereby the fighter overwhelms his assailant with a flurry of full speed, full-force blows.

conditioning training—A CFA training methodology requiring the practitioner to deliver a variety of offensive and defensive combinations for a 4-minute period. See proficiency training and street training.

contact evasion—Physically moving or manipulating your body to avoid being tackled by the adversary.

Contemporary Fighting Arts—A modern martial art and self-defense system made up of three parts: physical, mental, and spiritual.

conventional ground-fighting tools—Specific ground-fighting techniques designed to control, restrain, and temporarily incapacitate your adversary. Some conventional ground fighting tactics include: submission holds, locks, certain choking techniques, and specific striking techniques.

coordination—A physical attribute characterized by the ability to perform a technique or movement with efficiency, balance, and accuracy.

counterattack—Offensive action made to counter an assailant's initial attack.

courage—A combative attribute. The state of mind and spirit that enables a fighter to face danger and vicissitudes with confidence, resolution, and bravery.

creatine monohydrate—A tasteless and odorless white powder that mimics some of the effects of anabolic steroids. Creatine is a safe body-building product that can benefit anyone who wants to increase their strength, endurance, and lean muscle mass.

criminal awareness—One of the three categories of CFA awareness. It involves a general understanding and knowledge of the nature and dynamics of a criminal's motivations, mentalities, methods, and capabilities to perpetrate violent crime. See situational awareness and self-awareness.

criminal justice—The study of criminal law and the procedures associated with its enforcement.

criminology—The scientific study of crime and criminals.

cross-stepping—The process of crossing one foot in front of or behind the other when moving.

crushing tactics—Nuclear grappling-range techniques designed to crush the assailant's anatomical targets.

cue word - a unique word or personal statement that helps focus your attention on the execution of a skill, instead of its outcome.

# D

deadly force—Weapons or techniques that may result in unconsciousness, permanent disfigurement, or death.

deception—A combative attribute. A stratagem whereby you delude your assailant.

decisiveness—A combative attribute. The ability to follow a tactical course of action that is unwavering and focused.

defense—The ability to strategically thwart an assailant's attack (armed or unarmed).

defensive flow—A progression of continuous defensive responses.

defensive mentality—A defensive mind-set.

defensive reaction time—The elapsed time between an assailant's physical attack and your defensive response to that attack. See offensive reaction time.

demeanor—A person's outward behavior. One of the essential factors to consider when assessing a threatening individual.

diet—A lifestyle of healthy eating.

disingenuous vocalization—The strategic and deceptive

utilization of words to successfully launch a preemptive strike at your adversary.

distancing—The ability to quickly understand spatial relationships and how they relate to combat.

distractionary tactics—Various verbal and physical tactics designed to distract your adversary.

double-end bag—A small leather ball hung from the ceiling and anchored to the floor with bungee cord. It helps develop striking accuracy, speed, timing, eye-hand coordination, footwork and overall defensive skills.

double-leg takedown—A takedown that occurs when your opponent shoots for both of your legs to force you to the ground.

# E

ectomorph—One of the three somatotypes. A body type characterized by a high degree of slenderness, angularity, and fragility. See endomorph and mesomorph.

effectiveness—One of the three criteria for a CFA body weapon, technique, tactic, or maneuver. It means the ability to produce a desired effect. See efficiency and safety.

efficiency—One of the three criteria for a CFA body weapon, technique, tactic, or maneuver. It means the ability to reach an objective quickly and economically. See effectiveness and safety.

emotionless—A combative attribute. Being temporarily devoid of human feeling.

endomorph—One of the three somatotypes. A body type characterized by a high degree of roundness, softness, and body fat. See ectomorph and mesomorph.

evasion—A defensive maneuver that allows you to strategically maneuver your body away from the assailant's strike.

evasive sidestepping—Evasive footwork where the practitioner moves to either the right or left side.

evasiveness—A combative attribute. The ability to avoid threat or danger.

excessive force—An amount of force that exceeds the need for a particular event and is unjustified in the eyes of the law.

experimentation—The painstaking process of testing a combative hypothesis or theory.

explosiveness—A combative attribute that is characterized by a sudden outburst of violent energy.

# F

fear—A strong and unpleasant emotion caused by the anticipation or awareness of threat or danger. There are three stages of fear in order of intensity: fright, panic, and terror. See fright, panic, and terror.

feeder—A skilled technician who manipulates the focus mitts.

femoral nerve—A pressure point area located approximately 6 inches above the knee on the inside of the thigh.

fighting stance—Any one of the stances used in CFA's system. A strategic posture you can assume when face-to-face with an unarmed assailant(s). The fighting stance is generally used after you have launched your first-strike tool.

fight-or-flight syndrome—A response of the sympathetic nervous system to a fearful and threatening situation, during which it prepares your body to either fight or flee from the perceived danger.

finesse—A combative attribute. The ability to skillfully execute a movement or a series of movements with grace and refinement.

first strike—Proactive force used to interrupt the initial stages of an assault before it becomes a self-defense situation.

first-strike principle—A CFA principle that states that when physical danger is imminent and you have no other tactical option but to fight back, you should strike first, strike fast, and strike with authority and keep the pressure on.

first-strike stance—One of the stances used in CFA's system. A strategic posture used prior to initiating a first strike.

first-strike tools—Specific offensive tools designed to initiate a preemptive strike against your adversary.

fisted blows – Hand blows delivered with a clenched fist.

five tactical options – The five strategic responses you can make in a self-defense situation, listed in order of increasing level of resistance: comply, escape, de-escalate, assert, and fight back.

flexibility—The muscles' ability to move through maximum natural ranges. See muscular/skeletal conditioning.

focus mitts—Durable leather hand mitts used to develop and sharpen offensive and defensive skills.

footwork—Quick, economical steps performed on the balls of the feet while you are relaxed, alert, and balanced. Footwork is structured around four general movements: forward, backward, right, and left.

fractal tool—Offensive or defensive tools that can be used in more than one combat range.

fright—The first stage of fear; quick and sudden fear. See panic and terror.

full Beat – One of the four beat classifications in the Widow Maker Program. The full beat strike has a complete initiation and retraction phase.

# G

going postal - a slang term referring to a person who suddenly and unexpectedly attacks you with an explosive and frenzied flurry of blows. Also known as postal attack.

grappling range—One of the three ranges of unarmed combat. Grappling range is the closest distance of unarmed combat from which you can employ a wide variety of close-quarter tools and techniques. The grappling range of unarmed combat is also divided into two planes: vertical (standing) and horizontal (ground fighting). See kicking range and punching range.

grappling-range tools—The various body tools and techniques that are employed in the grappling range of unarmed combat, including head butts; biting, tearing, clawing, crushing, and gouging tactics; foot stomps, horizontal, vertical, and diagonal elbow strikes, vertical and diagonal knee strikes, chokes, strangles, joint locks, and holds. See punching range tools and kicking range tools.

ground fighting—Also known as the horizontal grappling plane, this is fighting that takes place on the ground.

guard—Also known as the hand guard, this refers to a fighter's hand positioning.

guard position—Also known as leg guard or scissors hold, this is a ground-fighting position in which a fighter is on his back holding his opponent between his legs.

# H

half beat – One of the four beat classifications in the Widow Maker Program. The half beat strike is delivered through the retraction phase of the proceeding strike.

hand positioning—See guard.

hand wraps—Long strips of cotton that are wrapped around the hands and wrists for greater protection.

haymaker—A wild and telegraphed swing of the arms executed by an unskilled fighter.

head-hunter—A fighter who primarily attacks the head.

heavy bag—A large cylindrical bag used to develop kicking, punching, or striking power.

high-line kick—One of the two different classifications of a kick. A kick that is directed to targets above an assailant's waist level. See low-line kick.

hip fusing—A full-contact drill that teaches a fighter to "stand his ground" and overcome the fear of exchanging blows with a stronger opponent. This exercise is performed by connecting two fighters with a 3-foot chain, forcing them to fight in the punching range of unarmed combat.

histrionics—The field of theatrics or acting.

hook kick—A circular kick that can be delivered in both kicking and punching ranges.

hook punch—A circular punch that can be delivered in both the punching and grappling ranges.

# I

impact power—Destructive force generated by mass and velocity.

impact training—A training exercise that develops pain tolerance.

incapacitate—To disable an assailant by rendering him unconscious or damaging his bones, joints, or organs.

initiative—Making the first offensive move in combat.

inside position—The area between the opponent's arms, where he has the greatest amount of control.

intent—One of the essential factors to consider when assessing a threatening individual. The assailant's purpose or motive. See demeanor, positioning, range, and weapon capability.

intuition—The innate ability to know or sense something without the use of rational thought.

# J

jersey Pull – Strategically pulling the assailant's shirt or jacket over his head as he disengages from the clinch position.

joint lock—A grappling-range technique that immobilizes the assailant's joint.

# K

kick—A sudden, forceful strike with the foot.

kicking range—One of the three ranges of unarmed combat. Kicking range is the furthest distance of unarmed combat wherein you use your legs to strike an assailant. See grappling range and punching range.

kicking-range tools—The various body weapons employed in the kicking range of unarmed combat, including side kicks, push kicks, hook kicks, and vertical kicks.

killer instinct—A cold, primal mentality that surges to your consciousness and turns you into a vicious fighter.

kinesics—The study of nonlinguistic body movement communications. (For example, eye movement, shrugs, or facial gestures.)

kinesiology—The study of principles and mechanics of human movement.

kinesthetic perception—The ability to accurately feel your body during the execution of a particular movement.

knowledge—One of the three factors that determine who will win a street fight. Knowledge means knowing and understanding how to fight. See skills and attitude.

# L

lead side -The side of the body that faces an assailant.

leg guard—See guard position.

linear movement—Movements that follow the path of a straight line.

low-maintenance tool—Offensive and defensive tools that require the least amount of training and practice to maintain proficiency. Low maintenance tools generally do not require preliminary stretching.

low-line kick—One of the two different classifications of a kick. A kick that is directed to targets below the assailant's waist level. (See high-line kick.)

lock—See joint lock.

# M

maneuver—To manipulate into a strategically desired position.

MAP—An acronym that stands for moderate, aggressive, passive. MAP provides the practitioner with three possible responses to various grabs, chokes, and holds that occur from a standing position. See aggressive response, moderate response, and passive response.

Marathon des Sables (MdS) - a six-day, 156-mile ultramarathon held in southern Morocco, in the Sahara Desert. It is considered by many to be the toughest footrace on earth.

martial arts—The "arts of war."

masking—The process of concealing your true feelings from your opponent by manipulating and managing your body language.

mechanics—(See body mechanics.)

mental toughness - a performance mechanism utilizing a collection of mental attributes that allow a person to cope, perform and prevail through the stress of extreme adversity.

mental component—One of the three vital components of the CFA system. The mental component includes the cerebral aspects of fighting including the killer instinct, strategic and tactical development, analysis and integration, philosophy, and cognitive development. See physical component and spiritual component.

mesomorph—One of the three somatotypes. A body type classified by a high degree of muscularity and strength. The mesomorph possesses the ideal physique for unarmed combat. See ectomorph and endomorph.

mobility—A combative attribute. The ability to move your body quickly and freely while balanced. See footwork.

moderate response—One of the three possible counters when assaulted by a grab, choke, or hold from a standing position. Moderate response requires you to counter your opponent with a control and restraint (submission hold). See aggressive response and passive response.

modern martial art—A pragmatic combat art that has evolved to meet the demands and characteristics of the present time.

mounted position—A dominant ground-fighting position where a fighter straddles his opponent.

muscular endurance—The muscles' ability to perform the same

motion or task repeatedly for a prolonged period of time.

muscular flexibility—The muscles' ability to move through maximum natural ranges.

muscular strength—The maximum force that can be exerted by a particular muscle or muscle group against resistance.

muscular/skeletal conditioning—An element of physical fitness that entails muscular strength, endurance, and flexibility.

# N

naked choke—A throat choke executed from the chest to back position. This secure choke is executed with two hands and it can be performed while standing, kneeling, and ground fighting with the opponent.

neck crush – A powerful pain compliance technique used when the adversary buries his head in your chest to avoid being razed.

neutralize—See incapacitate.

neutral zone—The distance outside the kicking range at which neither the practitioner nor the assailant can touch the other.

nonaggressive physiology—Strategic body language used prior to initiating a first strike.

nontelegraphic movement—Body mechanics or movements that do not inform an assailant of your intentions.

nuclear ground-fighting tools—Specific grappling range tools designed to inflict immediate and irreversible damage. Nuclear tools and tactics include biting tactics, tearing tactics, crushing tactics, continuous choking tactics, gouging techniques, raking tactics, and all striking techniques.

# O

offense—The armed and unarmed means and methods of attacking a criminal assailant.

offensive flow—Continuous offensive movements (kicks, blows, and strikes) with unbroken continuity that ultimately neutralize or terminate the opponent. See compound attack.

offensive reaction time—The elapsed time between target selection and target impaction.

one-mindedness—A state of deep concentration wherein you are free from all distractions (internal and external).

ostrich defense—One of the biggest mistakes one can make when defending against an opponent. This is when the practitioner looks away from that which he fears (punches, kicks, and strikes). His mentality is, "If I can't see it, it can't hurt me."

# P

pain tolerance—Your ability to physically and psychologically withstand pain.

panic—The second stage of fear; overpowering fear. See fright and terror.

parry—A defensive technique: a quick, forceful slap that redirects an assailant's linear attack. There are two types of parries: horizontal and vertical.

passive response—One of the three possible counters when assaulted by a grab, choke, or hold from a standing position. Passive response requires you to nullify the assault without injuring your adversary. See aggressive response and moderate response.

patience—A combative attribute. The ability to endure and tolerate difficulty.

perception—Interpretation of vital information acquired from your senses when faced with a potentially threatening situation.

philosophical resolution—The act of analyzing and answering various questions concerning the use of violence in defense of yourself and others.

philosophy—One of the five aspects of CFA's mental component. A deep state of introspection whereby you methodically resolve critical questions concerning the use of force in defense of yourself or others.

physical attributes—The numerous physical qualities that enhance your combative skills and abilities.

physical component—One of the three vital components of the CFA system. The physical component includes the physical aspects of fighting, such as physical fitness, weapon/technique mastery, and combative attributes. See mental component and spiritual component.

physical conditioning—See combative fitness.

physical fitness—See combative fitness.

positional asphyxia—The arrangement, placement, or positioning of your opponent's body in such a way as to interrupt your breathing and cause unconsciousness or possibly death.

positioning—The spatial relationship of the assailant to the assailed person in terms of target exposure, escape, angle of attack, and various other strategic considerations.

postal attack - see going postal.

power—A physical attribute of armed and unarmed combat. The amount of force you can generate when striking an anatomical target.

power generators—Specific points on your body that generate impact power. There are three anatomical power generators: shoulders, hips, and feet.

precision—See accuracy.

preemptive strike—See first strike.

premise—An axiom, concept, rule, or any other valid reason to modify or go beyond that which has been established.

preparedness—A state of being ready for combat. There are three components of preparedness: affective preparedness, cognitive preparedness, and psychomotor preparedness.

probable reaction dynamics - The opponent's anticipated or predicted movements or actions during both armed and unarmed combat.

proficiency training—A CFA training methodology requiring the practitioner to execute a specific body weapon, technique, maneuver, or tactic over and over for a prescribed number of repetitions. See conditioning training and street training.

proxemics—The study of the nature and effect of man's personal space.

proximity—The ability to maintain a strategically safe distance from a threatening individual.

pseudospeciation—A combative attribute. The tendency to assign subhuman and inferior qualities to a threatening assailant.

psychological conditioning—The process of conditioning the mind for the horrors and rigors of real combat.

psychomotor preparedness—One of the three components of preparedness. Psychomotor preparedness means possessing all of the physical skills and attributes necessary to defeat a formidable adversary. See affective preparedness and cognitive preparedness.

punch—A quick, forceful strike of the fists.

punching range—One of the three ranges of unarmed combat. Punching range is the mid range of unarmed combat from which the fighter uses his hands to strike his assailant. See kicking range and grappling range.

punching-range tools—The various body weapons that are employed in the punching range of unarmed combat, including finger jabs, palm-heel strikes, rear cross, knife-hand strikes, horizontal and shovel hooks, uppercuts, and hammer-fist strikes. See grappling-range tools and kicking-range tools.

# Q

qualities of combat—See attributes of combat.

quarter beat - One of the four beat classifications of the Widow Maker Program. Quarter beat strikes never break contact with the assailant's face. Quarter beat strikes are primarily responsible for creating the psychological panic and trauma when Razing.

# R

range—The spatial relationship between a fighter and a threatening assailant.

range deficiency—The inability to effectively fight and defend in all ranges of combat (armed and unarmed).

range manipulation—A combative attribute. The strategic manipulation of combat ranges.

range proficiency—A combative attribute. The ability to effectively fight and defend in all ranges of combat (armed and unarmed).

ranges of engagement—See combat ranges.

ranges of unarmed combat—The three distances (kicking range, punching range, and grappling range) a fighter might physically engage with an assailant while involved in unarmed combat.

raze – To level, demolish or obliterate.

razer – One who performs the Razing methodology.

razing – The second phase of the Widow Maker Program. A series of vicious close quarter techniques designed to physically and psychologically extirpate a criminal attacker.

razing amplifier - a technique, tactic or procedure that magnifies the destructiveness of your razing technique.

reaction dynamics—see probable reaction dynamics.

reaction time—The elapsed time between a stimulus and the response to that particular stimulus. See offensive reaction time and defensive reaction time.

rear cross—A straight punch delivered from the rear hand that crosses from right to left (if in a left stance) or left to right (if in a right stance).

rear side—The side of the body furthest from the assailant. See lead side.

reasonable force—That degree of force which is not excessive for a particular event and which is appropriate in protecting yourself or others.

refinement—The strategic and methodical process of improving or perfecting.

relocation principle—Also known as relocating, this is a street-fighting tactic that requires you to immediately move to a new location (usually by flanking your adversary) after delivering a compound attack.

repetition—Performing a single movement, exercise, strike, or action continuously for a specific period.

research—A scientific investigation or inquiry.

rhythm—Movements characterized by the natural ebb and flow of related elements.

ritual-oriented training—Formalized training that is conducted without intrinsic purpose. See combat-oriented training and sport-oriented training.

# S

safety—One of the three criteria for a CFA body weapon, technique, maneuver, or tactic. It means that the tool, technique, maneuver or tactic provides the least amount of danger and risk for the practitioner. See efficiency and effectiveness.

scissors hold—See guard position.

scorching – Quickly and inconspicuously applying oleoresin capsicum (hot pepper extract) on your fingertips and then razing your adversary.

self-awareness—One of the three categories of CFA awareness. Knowing and understanding yourself. This includes aspects of yourself which may provoke criminal violence and which will promote a proper and strong reaction to an attack. See criminal awareness and situational awareness.

self-confidence—Having trust and faith in yourself.

self-enlightenment—The state of knowing your capabilities, limitations, character traits, feelings, general attributes, and motivations. See self-awareness.

set—A term used to describe a grouping of repetitions.

shadow fighting—A CFA training exercise used to develop and refine your tools, techniques, and attributes of armed and unarmed combat.

sharking – A counter attack technique that is used when your adversary grabs your razing hand.

shielding wedge - a defensive maneuver used to counter an unarmed postal attack.

situational awareness—One of the three categories of CFA awareness. A state of being totally alert to your immediate surroundings, including people, places, objects, and actions. (See criminal awareness and self-awareness.)

skeletal alignment—The proper alignment or arrangement of your body. Skeletal alignment maximizes the structural integrity of striking tools.

skills—One of the three factors that determine who will win a street fight. Skills refers to psychomotor proficiency with the tools and techniques of combat. See Attitude and Knowledge.

slipping—A defensive maneuver that permits you to avoid an assailant's linear blow without stepping out of range. Slipping can be accomplished by quickly snapping the head and upper torso sideways (right or left) to avoid the blow.

snap back—A defensive maneuver that permits you to avoid an assailant's linear and circular blows without stepping out of range. The snap back can be accomplished by quickly snapping the head backward to avoid the assailant's blow.

somatotypes—A method of classifying human body types or builds into three different categories: endomorph, mesomorph, and ectomorph. See endomorph, mesomorph, and ectomorph.

sparring—A training exercise where two or more fighters fight each other while wearing protective equipment.

speed—A physical attribute of armed and unarmed combat. The rate or a measure of the rapid rate of motion.

spiritual component—One of the three vital components of the CFA system. The spiritual component includes the metaphysical issues and aspects of existence. See physical component and mental component.

sport-oriented training—Training that is geared for competition and governed by a set of rules. See combat-oriented training and ritual-oriented training.

sprawling—A grappling technique used to counter a double- or single-leg takedown.

square off—To be face-to-face with a hostile or threatening assailant who is about to attack you.

stance—One of the many strategic postures you assume prior to or during armed or unarmed combat.

stick fighting—Fighting that takes place with either one or two sticks.

strategic positioning—Tactically positioning yourself to either escape, move behind a barrier, or use a makeshift weapon.

strategic/tactical development—One of the five elements of CFA's mental component.

strategy—A carefully planned method of achieving your goal of engaging an assailant under advantageous conditions.

street fight—A spontaneous and violent confrontation between two or more individuals wherein no rules apply.

street fighter—An unorthodox combatant who has no formal training. His combative skills and tactics are usually developed in the street by the process of trial and error.

street training—A CFA training methodology requiring the practitioner to deliver explosive compound attacks for 10 to 20 seconds. See condition ng training and proficiency training.

strength training—The process of developing muscular strength through systematic application of progressive resistance.

stress - physiological and psychological arousal caused by a stressor.

stressors - any activity, situation, circumstance, event, experience, or condition that causes a person to experience both physiological and psychological stress.

striking art—A combat art that relies predominantly on striking techniques to neutralize or terminate a criminal attacker.

striking shield—A rectangular shield constructed of foam and vinyl used to develop power in your kicks, punches, and strikes.

striking tool—A natural body weapon that impacts with the assailant's anatomical target.

strong side—The strongest and most coordinated side of your body.

structure—A definite and organized pattern.

style—The distinct manner in which a fighter executes or performs his combat skills.

stylistic integration—The purposeful and scientific collection of tools and techniques from various disciplines, which are strategically integrated and dramatically altered to meet three essential criteria: efficiency, effectiveness, and combative safety.

submission holds—Also known as control and restraint techniques, many of these locks and holds create sufficient pain to cause the adversary to submit.

system—The unification of principles, philosophies, rules, strategies, methodologies, tools, and techniques of a particular method of combat.

# T

tactic—The skill of using the available means to achieve an end.

target awareness—A combative attribute that encompasses five strategic principles: target orientation, target recognition, target selection, target impaction, and target exploitation.

target exploitation—A combative attribute. The strategic maximization of your assailant's reaction dynamics during a fight. Target exploitation can be applied in both armed and unarmed encounters.

target impaction—The successful striking of the appropriate anatomical target.

target orientation—A combative attribute. Having a workable knowledge of the assailant's anatomical targets.

target recognition—The ability to immediately recognize appropriate anatomical targets during an emergency self-defense situation.

target selection—The process of mentally selecting the appropriate anatomical target for your self-defense situation. This is predicated on certain factors, including proper force response, assailant's positioning, and range.

target stare—A form of telegraphing in which you stare at the anatomical target you intend to strike.

target zones—The three areas in which an assailant's anatomical targets are located. (See zone one, zone two and zone three.)

technique—A systematic procedure by which a task is accomplished.

telegraphic cognizance—A combative attribute. The ability to recognize both verbal and non-verbal signs of aggression or assault.

telegraphing—Unintentionally making your intentions known to your adversary.

tempo—The speed or rate at which you speak.

terminate—To kill.

terror—The third stage of fear; defined as overpowering fear. See fright and panic.

timing—A physical and mental attribute of armed and unarmed combat. Your ability to execute a movement at the optimum moment.

tone—The overall quality or character of your voice.

tool—See body weapon.

traditional martial arts—Any martial art that fails to evolve and change to meet the demands and characteristics of its present environment.

traditional style/system—See traditional martial arts.

training drills—The various exercises and drills aimed at perfecting combat skills, attributes, and tactics.

trap and tuck – A counter move technique used when the adversary attempts to raze you during your quarter beat assault.

# U

unified mind—A mind free and clear of distractions and focused on the combative situation.

use of force response—A combative attribute. Selecting the appropriate level of force for a particular emergency self-defense situation.

# V

viciousness—A combative attribute. The propensity to be extremely violent and destructive often characterized by intense savagery.

violence—The intentional utilization of physical force to coerce, injure, cripple, or kill.

visualization—Also known as mental visualization or mental imagery. The purposeful formation of mental images and scenarios in the mind's eye.

# W

warm-up—A series of mild exercises, stretches, and movements designed to prepare you for more intense exercise.

weak side—The weaker and more uncoordinated side of your body.

weapon and technique mastery—A component of CFA's physical component. The kinesthetic and psychomotor development of a weapon or combative technique.

weapon capability—An assailant's ability to use and attack with a particular weapon.

webbing - The first phase of the Widow Maker Program. Webbing is a two hand strike delivered to the assailant's chin. It is called Webbing because your hands resemble a large web that wraps around the enemy's face.

widow maker - One who makes widows by destroying husbands.

widow maker program – A CFA combat program specifically designed to teach the law abiding citizen how to use extreme force when faced with immediate threat of unlawful deadly criminal attack. The Widow Maker program is divided into two phases or methodologies: Webbing and Razing.

# Y

yell—A loud and aggressive scream or shout used for various strategic reasons.

# Z

zero beat – One of the four beat classifications of the Widow Maker, Feral Fighting and Savage Street Fighting Programs. Zero beat strikes are full pressure techniques applied to a specific target until it completely ruptures. They include gouging, crushing, biting, and choking techniques.

zone one—Anatomical targets related to your senses, including the eyes, temple, nose, chin, and back of neck.

zone three—Anatomical targets related to your mobility, including thighs, knees, shins, and instep.

zone two—Anatomical targets related to your breathing, including front of neck, solar plexus, ribs, and groin.

# About Sammy Franco

With over 30 years of experience, Sammy Franco is one of the world's foremost authorities on armed and unarmed self-defense. Highly regarded as a leading innovator in combat sciences, Mr. Franco was one of the premier pioneers in the field of "reality-based" self-defense and combat instruction.

Sammy Franco is perhaps best known as the founder and creator of Contemporary Fighting Arts (CFA), a state-of-the-art offensive-based combat system that is specifically designed for real-world self-defense. CFA is a sophisticated and practical system of self-defense, designed specifically to provide efficient and effective methods to avoid, defuse, confront, and neutralize both armed and unarmed attackers.

Sammy Franco has frequently been featured in martial art magazines, newspapers, and appeared on numerous radio and television programs. Mr. Franco has also authored numerous books, magazine articles, and editorials and has developed a popular library of instructional videos.

Sammy Franco's experience and credibility in the combat science is unequaled. One of his many accomplishments in this field includes the fact that he has earned the ranking of a Law Enforcement Master Instructor, and has designed, implemented, and taught officer survival training to the United States Border Patrol (USBP). He has instructed members of the US Secret Service, Military Special Forces,

Washington DC Police Department, Montgomery County, Maryland Deputy Sheriffs, and the US Library of Congress Police. Sammy Franco is also a member of the prestigious International Law Enforcement Educators and Trainers Association (ILEETA) as well as the American Society of Law Enforcement Trainers (ASLET) and he is listed in the "Who's Who Director of Law Enforcement Instructors."

Sammy Franco is also a nationally certified Law Enforcement Instructor in the following curricula: PR-24 Side-Handle Baton, Police Arrest and Control Procedures, Police Personal Weapons Tactics, Police Power Handcuffing Methods, Police Oleoresin Capsicum Aerosol Training (OCAT), Police Weapon Retention and Disarming Methods, Police Edged Weapon Countermeasures and "Use of Force" Assessment and Response Methods.

Mr. Franco regularly conducts dynamic and enlightening seminars on different aspects of combat training, mental toughness and achieving personal peak performance.

On a personal level, Sammy Franco is an animal lover, who will go to great lengths to assist and rescue animals. Throughout the years, he's rescued everything from turkey vultures to goats. However, his most treasured moments are always spent with his beloved German Shepherd dogs.

For more information about Mr. Franco, you can visit his website at **SammyFranco.com** or follow him on Twitter **@RealSammyFranco**

# Other Books by Sammy Franco

## HEAVY BAG COMBINATIONS
### The Ultimate Guide to Heavy Bag Punching Combinations
*by Sammy Franco*

Heavy Bag Combinations is the second book in Sammy Franco's best-selling Heavy Bag Training Series. With over 300+ photographs and detailed step-by-step instructions, Heavy Bag Combinations provides beginner, intermediate and advanced heavy bag workout combinations that will challenge you for the rest of your life! In fact, even the most experienced athlete will advance his fighting skills to the next level and beyond. 8.5 x 5.5, paperback, photos, illus, 248 pages.

## THE COMPLETE BODY OPPONENT BAG BOOK
*by Sammy Franco*

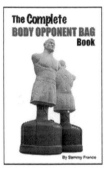

In this one-of-a-kind book, Sammy Franco teaches you the many hidden training features of the body opponent bag that will improve your fighting skills and boost your conditioning. With detailed photographs, step-by-step instructions, and dozens of unique workout routines, The Complete Body Opponent Bag Book is the authoritative resource for mastering this lifelike punching bag. It covers stances, punching, kicking, grappling techniques, mobility and footwork, targets, fighting ranges, training gear, time based workouts, punching and kicking combinations, weapons training, grappling drills, ground fighting, and dozens of workouts. 8.5 x 5.5, paperback, 139 photos, illustrations, 206 pages.

## INVINCIBLE
### Mental Toughness Techniques for Peak Performance
*by Sammy Franco*

Invincible is a treasure trove of battle-tested techniques and strategies for improving mental toughness in all aspects of life. It teaches you how to unlock the true power of your mind and achieve success in sports, fitness, high-risk professions, self-defense, and other peak performance activities. However, you don't have to be an athlete or warrior to benefit from this unique mental toughness book. In fact, the mental skills featured in this indispensable program can be used by anyone who wants to reach their full potential in life. 8.5 x 5.5, paperback, photos, illus, 250 pages.

## THE WIDOW MAKER PROGRAM
### Extreme Self-Defense for Deadly Force Situations
#### by Sammy Franco

The Widow Maker Program is a shocking and revolutionary fighting style designed to unleash extreme force when faced with the immediate threat of an unlawful deadly criminal attack. In this unique book, self-defense innovator Sammy Franco teaches you his brutal and unorthodox combat style that is virtually indefensible and utterly devastating. With over 250 photographs and detailed step-by-step instructions, The Widow Maker Program teaches you Franco's surreptitious Webbing and Razing techniques. When combined, these two fighting methods create an unstoppable force capable of destroying the toughest adversary. 8.5 x 5.5, paperback, photos, illus, 218 pages.

## FERAL FIGHTING
### Advanced Widow Maker Fighting Techniques
#### by Sammy Franco

In this sequel, Sammy Franco marches forward with cutting-edge concepts and techniques that will take your self-defense skills to entirely new levels of combat performance. Feral Fighting includes Franco's revolutionary Shielding Wedge technique. When used correctly, it transforms you into an unstoppable human meat grinder, capable of destroying any criminal adversary. Feral Fighting also teaches you the cunning art or Scorching. Learn how to convert your fingertips into burning torches that generate over 2 million scoville heat units causing excruciating pain and temporarily blindness. 8.5 x 5.5, paperback, photos, illustrations, 204 pages.

## MAXIMUM DAMAGE
### Hidden Secrets Behind Brutal Fighting Combination
#### by Sammy Franco

Maximum Damage teaches you the quickest ways to beat your opponent in the street by exploiting his physical and psychological reactions in a fight. Learn how to stay two steps ahead of your adversary by knowing exactly how he will react to your strikes before they are delivered. In this unique book, reality based self-defense expert Sammy Franco reveals his unique Probable Reaction Dynamic (PRD) fighting method. Probable reaction dynamics are both a scientific and comprehensive offensive strategy based on the positional theory of combat. Regardless of your style of fighting, PRD training will help you overpower your opponent by seamlessly integrating your strikes into brutal fighting combinations that are fast, ferocious and final! 8.5 x 5.5, paperback, 240 photos, illustrations, 238 pages.

## SAVAGE STREET FIGHTING
### Tactical Savagery as a Last Resort
*by Sammy Franco*

In this revolutionary book, Sammy Franco reveals the science behind his most primal street fighting method. Savage Street Fighting is a brutal self-defense system specifically designed to teach the law-abiding citizen how to use "Tactical Savagery" when faced with the immediate threat of an unlawful deadly criminal attack. Savage Street Fighting is systematically engineered to protect you when there are no other self-defense options left! With over 300 photographs and detailed step-by-step instructions, Savage Street Fighting is a must-have book for anyone concerned about real world self-defense. Now is the time to learn how to unleash your inner beast! 8.5 x 5.5, paperback, 317 photos, illustrations, 232 pages.

## FIRST STRIKE
### End a Fight in Ten Seconds or Less!
*by Sammy Franco*

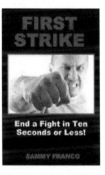

Learn how to stop any attack before it starts by mastering the art of the preemptive strike. First Strike gives you an easy-to-learn yet highly effective self-defense game plan for handling violent close-quarter combat encounters. First Strike will teach you instinctive, practical and realistic self-defense techniques that will drop any criminal attacker to the floor with one punishing blow. By reading this book and by practicing, you will learn the hard-hitting skills necessary to execute a punishing first strike and ultimately prevail in a self-defense situation. And that's what it is all about: winning in as little time as possible. 8.5 x 5.5, paperback, photos, illustrations, 202 pages.

## WAR MACHINE
### How to Transform Yourself Into A Vicious & Deadly Street Fighter
*by Sammy Franco*

War Machine is a book that will change you for the rest of your life! When followed accordingly, War Machine will forge your mind, body and spirit into iron. Once armed with the mental and physical attributes of the War Machine, you will become a strong and confident warrior that can handle just about anything that life may throw your way. In essence, War Machine is a way of life. Powerful, intense, and hard. 11 x 8.5, paperback, photos, illustrations, 210 pages.

## KUBOTAN POWER
### Quick and Simple Steps to Mastering the Kubotan Keychain
*by Sammy Franco*

With over 290 photographs and step-by-step instructions, Kubotan Power is the authoritative resource for mastering this devastating self-defense weapon. In this one-of-a-kind book, world-renowned self-defense expert, Sammy Franco takes thirty years of real-world teaching experience and gives you quick, easy and practical kubotan techniques that can be used by civilians, law enforcement personnel, or military professionals. The Kubotan is an incredible self-defense weapon that has helped thousands of people effectively defend themselves. Men, women, law enforcement officers, military, and security professionals alike, appreciate this small and discreet self-defense tool. Unfortunately, however, very little has been written about the kubotan, leaving it shrouded in both mystery and ignorance. As a result, most people don't know how to unleash the full power of this unique personal defense weapon. 8.5 x 5.5, paperback, 290 photos, illustrations, 204 pages.

## CONTEMPORARY FIGHTING ARTS, LLC
### "Real World Self-Defense Since 1989"
### www.SammyFranco.com

162

# Finis

74591707R00097

Made in the USA
Middletown, DE
27 May 2018